Beyond the Goalcrease:
Wit & Wisdom on Life Between the Pipes from Former NHL Netminder Robb Stauber

by
Robb Stauber with Ross Bernstein

Beyond the Goalcrease:
Wit & Wisdom on Life Between the Pipes from Former NHL Netminder Robb Stauber

by Robb Stauber with Ross Bernstein

ISBN#: 0-9634871-8-3

To learn more about any of nearly 30 books which Ross Bernstein has written, please visit his website at: *WWW.BERNSTEINBOOKS.COM*

Book Cover Painting by Artist Tim Cortes:
TIMCORTESART.COM

*To order a limited edition print of the cover painting, please contact the Goalcrease.

Distributed by Adventure Publications,
Cambridge, MN (800) 678-7006

Printed by Printing Enterprises: New Brighton, MN

Photos courtesy of: Robb Stauber, the L.A. Kings, Buffalo Sabres, Minnesota Wild, USA Hockey, the University of Minnesota Men's Athletics Dept., Mike Staff and P&H Creative Group

A portion of the proceeds from the sale of
this book will benefit the newly created:

"ROBB STAUBER SCHOLARSHIP FOUNDATION"

To learn more about the foundation
please contact the Goalcrease or visit their website at:

WWW.GOALCREASE.COM

Thank You For Your Support!

The Goalcrease
7435 Washington Avenue South
Edina, MN 55439
(952) 942-7001

For Ruby & Jaxson...

When Robb asked me to be part of his new goaltending book, I was thrilled to help him out. I first got to know Robb when we were teammates together back in the early 90's with the Los Angeles Kings. Robb had come off an outstanding college career with Minnesota and we welcomed his arrival. During Robb's career he suffered and overcame several serious injuries. Robb's work ethic and determination enabled him to battle his way back to being a consistent and reliable NHL goaltender.

Robb was a talented professional. He studied his opponents, was very prepared, and always gave his best effort. Whether it was a game or a practice, Robb's competitive spirit and intensity made us a better hockey club. In the 1993 Stanley Cup run, Robb came in and won us a couple of very big games. Teamed with Kelly Hrudey, they gave us goaltending we could count on.

Robb was definitely not boring in the net. He could, and did, make us all nervous many a night. Robb loved to charge out at opposing forwards, he loved to roam from his net and not only play the puck but sometimes even try to stickhandle around the opposition. In fact, (ESPN Radio host) Jim Rome actually nicknamed him "Blue Line." I would not have been surprised to see him try to take a face-off.

Watching young kids play and seeing young goalies come into the NHL, I believe Robb to be an excellent choice as a goaltender's coach or mentor. The importance and demands made on a goaltender in today's low scoring, tightly played game is enormous. Knowing Robb's preparation, intensity and love for the game, I believe Robb's academy and teaching would be invaluable to a young goaltender.

I am extremely happy for Robb that he is now teaching and coaching. I saw him as a teammate and as a winner both on and off the ice.

-- Wayne Gretzky --

I first met Robb back in the late 1980s when I had a silly notion to try out for the Gopher hockey team. After a brief "cup of coffee," however, I was promptly shown the door. But, as luck would have it, one of the cheerleaders told me that they were looking for a new team mascot, "Goldy the Gopher." She then explained to me that there were two pieces of criteria required for the job. First, you had to know how to skate and play hockey, and secondly, you had to be a complete idiot. I apparently fit on both accounts, and got the gig.

With that, I became the skating rodent at old Mariucci Arena. It was a blast. I got into a good deal of mischief, but had a lot of fun being able to still hang around the team and be a part of the action. During that time I also made a lot of good buddies and among them was Robb. As a friend, Robb is as down to earth as they come and is really just a great guy. As a player, Robb was so intense and unlike anything I had ever seen before. When he was in goal, all bets were off — it was show time. Other than maybe two heavy-weights squaring off toe-to-toe at center ice, nothing got the crowd more fired up than when Robb left his crease to challenge an opposing skater on a would-be breakaway. The result was usually a spectacular collision with the bewildered player sliding harmlessly down the ice on his back and Robb somehow winding up with the puck somewhere out near at the blue line. In a word, it was awesome.

Robb is so driven and so determined. I will never forget being at the Civic Center back in 1989 when the Gophers lost to Harvard in the NCAA Finals. Going from the elation of watching Randy Skarda nearly end it when he hit the pipe in overtime, to seeing Robb get beat shortly thereafter on a fluke bounce in front of the net was nothing short of heart-breaking. As a fan I was crushed. Devastated probably couldn't even come close to justifying how Robb was feeling at that very same moment. That is hockey though, and Robb bounced back through his positive attitude and mental toughness.

Robb changed the rules during his illustrious tenure in Gold Country and made us proud for more than a decade playing professional hockey too. We as Minnesotans love it when our local boys do good, and Robb, you dun' good my friend. What is even more impressive about Robb's accomplishments on the ice, are what he has done off the ice. Robb's lifelong dream of being able to operate his own goaltending academy finally came to fruition a few years ago when he opened the Goalcrease and the reviews have been nothing short of amazing.

It is only fitting that such a pioneer of the game go on to revolutionize the business of teaching and training as well. Robb's state-of-the-art facility in Edina is a goalie Mecca and is almost worth the drive over even if you don't know the difference between a blue line and a clothes line. He has assembled an incredible staff of experts to train kids of all ages and they are truly making a difference in the world of hockey.

Goaltending is such a specialized and unique position and it is about time that somebody had the guts to go out and create a year round academy where kids can go to better themselves. The fruits of Robb's labor are already being seen in his kids' teams winning championships from peewees to the pros. And, more and more of his protégés are reaching their full potential; making A teams; traveling teams; high school teams; junior teams; and earning college scholarships along the way. More importantly though they are having fun, and that is what it is all about.

Too many parents nowadays are spending a fortune on fancy goalie masks for their young kids, yet they don't bother to spend a dime on what really matters — learning and mastering the fundamentals of goaltending. Take my advice, if you have a son or daughter that is a goalie or wants to be a goalie, send them to the Goalcrease. It will be one of the best investments you could ever make in their future. Believe me, he is onto something very special over there.

As for the book, Robb also wanted to include not only his own ideas and philosophies on goaltending, but those of various other teachers and peers who he deeply respects, such as Barry Melrose, Bob Mason, Warren Strelow, Don Lucia, Doug Woog and Don Beaupre, among others. Because of that, I think the book is an invaluable resource for any hockey fan, regardless of if you are a goaltender or not. In fact, the book covers all the bases with regards to the lifestyle of goaltending and offers a ton of not only advice and guidance, but also tips and techniques for aspiring goalies, parents and hockey coaches.

So, I was extremely honored when Robb asked me to help write his life story. As the author of more than 30 books, this one ranks right up there with my all-time favorites. To be able to collaborate on a project like this with someone who I respect and admire so much was a real thrill. Then, to be able to get my boyhood idol Wayne Gretzky on board as well, that was just icing on the cake. With that, I give you "Beyond the Goalcrease," a story about a humble kid from Duluth who has truly changed the game. And more importantly, he has done it on his own terms — the right way. Congratulations on all of your success pal, you truly deserve it.

-- Ross Bernstein --

WELCOME!

First, I would like to thank some people who helped me to get to where I am at in life, because without them I would be nowhere. So, here is a heartfelt thank you to my family, my friends, my former teammates, all of my coaches through the years, and everybody here at the Goalcrease. You are the people closest to me who have taken an interest in my passion and for that I will be eternally grateful to your love and friendship. I would also like to thank all the people who took the time to be a part of this book, your insight was invaluable and I really appreciate it.

Putting this book together was so much fun. To be able to sit back and reflect was just wonderful, it forced me to reevaluate some things and to truly count my blessings. My hope is that this book will be able to shed some light on the trials and tribulations that goalies, both young and old, are subjected too — and then to help them to reach their potential.

Hopefully the book can be used as a tool for both parents as well as their sons or daughters to get better. That could mean better as a player; better as a coach; better as the parent of an athlete; and better as someone who is trying to improve themselves as a person. Hopefully my philosophies on hockey will be able to help people make the right choices in both athletics as well as in life. If I succeed in doing that, then the book will be a success.

Lastly, I just want to say how excited I am to have been able to work

with local author Ross Bernstein on this project. Ross has been a good friend over the years since our days at the University and someone who I am honored to have help write my story. We both share a love for the game of hockey and that is what brought us together on this project. It has taken us over a year to get it done, but I am certain that the finished product will make it all well worth the wait. I hope you have half as much fun reading it as we did putting it all together. Enjoy!

-- Robb Stauber --

CHAPTER ONE:
GROWING UP IN DULUTH

My name is Robert Thomas Stauber and I was born on November 25, 1967, in Duluth, Minnesota. I grew up in the Piedmont Heights area of West Duluth as the fifth of six kids: Dan, Jamie, John, Pete, myself and Bill. We all loved hockey and we all drove our parents nuts when it came to anything that had to do with hockey. Come on, what else is there to do up in Northern Minnesota in the dead of Winter?

We grew up very modestly in a hard working, middle-class family. My dad had a business where he was always on call to go out and fumigate big ocean-going ships in the Duluth harbor for pests and rodents. If a ship came in at 3:00 in the morning, he would have to get up and make sure that it was cleaned properly to pass U.S. customs inspections. He later got into janitorial supply sales for hospitals and schools. My mom worked outside the home as well, managing medical records for several area hospitals.

They both worked their tails off for all of us kids to give us opportunities that they didn't have. When they came home from work they were just dead tired and then they had six wild kids to deal with, so I couldn't imagine how tough that must have been. They just gave everything to their kids and sacrificed so much for us. I wouldn't even know how to begin to thank them for everything they did for me. Without a doubt, their six kids were far more important than anything else in their lives. They never bought anything new for themselves, they never took any trips, they just poured everything they had into the benefit of us and what we wanted to do. We did everything as a family too, whether it was camping trips or watching hockey, it was all about the family. They wanted us to have more opportunities and experiences than they did and for that I will forever be grateful to them.

My mom is just as tough as they come. Mentally, I haven't ever met

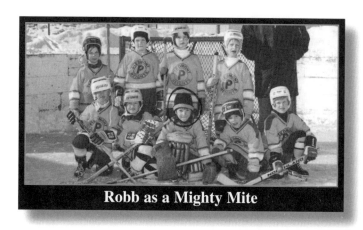
Robb as a Mighty Mite

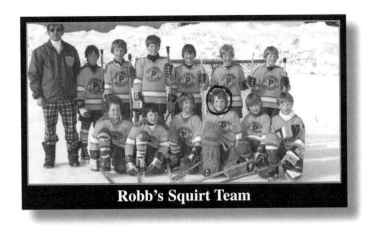

Robb's Squirt Team

anyone stronger than her. I would like to think that a lot of my mental toughness comes from her, she taught me a lot and really led by example for all of us kids. I mean, hey, six kids? Come on, you would have to be tough! She is also very smart and really taught me a lot about how to deal with conflict resolution. Now, when I get into an argument, I try to think things through ahead of time. I don't like conflict, but when it comes my way I try to be smart about it and take things in before I respond. I think that sort of methodical, deductive reasoning translates well in goaltending too. You have to be quick and responsive to whatever might come your way, but you also have to do your homework and really think things through ahead of time to have a good game plan.

Later in life, if I had a bad game and came home disappointed, my mom usually knew exactly what was wrong. She would usually tell me that my "head wasn't in it." She didn't care about the fundamentals of what went wrong, she just had that maternal instinct. She knew me well enough to know what my problems were and she didn't beat around the bush in telling me either. She knew if I was prepared or not because she knew me better than anybody. She would never yell or scream or anything like that either, it was always just a subtle comment or suggestion. And she never tried to make me feel better by making excuses or anything. That was not her. She just wanted me to look within myself to get better. If that meant working harder and paying attention better, than so be it.

Now, as far as my dad goes, all I can say is that you just wouldn't want to mess with him. Period. He was so principled, he just really stood by what he believed in. He also never got mad a lot, but when he did... watch out! He meant business. He is a great father though and someone I really look up to in life. As a person I know for sure that my parents shaped and influenced my philosophy on life. I also think a lot of that translated over into being a goaltender as well. So many of the values that I learned, such as hard work and dedication, came from them and the way they lived their lives.

My parents taught me to take responsibility for my own actions and that has really guided me throughout my entire life, both on and off the ice. They just knew what to say and when to say it to me at exactly the right times.

And most of the time, they didn't say a word, they just gave me a hug or a smile — which was oftentimes the best thing in the world for me to get. I think parents can learn so much from that. In fact, that might be the most important thing I have to say in this entire book, it is that important.

Even though I grew up playing baseball, football and golf, the common bond, or glue, that held my family together was hockey. We loved it. It didn't matter how cold or dark it was outside, we wanted to play. And when there was no ice, we banged heads in the basement and back yard. It was awesome. The age range between youngest and oldest child was just eight years, so there were some epic hockey games in the neighborhood between us brothers over the years. A lot of blood was spilled on that ice, let me tell ya. Come on, with six kids we had our own "Team Stauber!"

I can remember as a child our family used to house out-of-town kids who played hockey at the University of Minnesota-Duluth from time to time. I think my parents did it in exchange for free tickets, I am not sure, but for whatever the reason it was great. We got to see the Bulldogs play all the time down at the Duluth Arena, and we got to have a college hockey player hanging around the house who could show us cool moves and stuff down at the neighborhood rink. We would skate there all day and all night until our parents would come drag us off to go to bed so they could turn off the lights and flood the ice. I can remember just literally freezing my fingers and toes almost to the point of frostbite because I didn't want to come in off the ice. My dad used to have to rub my hands and toes to get the blood flowing back to them and warm me up, it used to burn so bad. But hey, that was hockey. And do you know what? We did that every day, we loved it. Playing outside in the wind and the cold made you tough. Playing in those conditions separated those who really loved the game from those who didn't. Plus, it was unlimited ice time, so we could stay out there as long as we wanted. Those were great memories and I wouldn't trade them for anything. I think a lot of who I am today was molded 30-plus years ago out on that rink.

As a kid growing up the second youngest of six brothers, I can tell you that being able to hang out with my older brothers motivated me. I didn't want to always be the little kid in the family and with hockey, that was the great equalizer. If I could skate with them, then I could hang out with them. That too, motivated me to try as hard as I could. Believe me, there was a lot of "I'll show you…" in my daily life and I was always trying to earn their respect. To be accepted by the older guys was just awesome and that was the ultimate motivating factor for me. I know that whole concept carried forward as I got

Robb, Kickin' it old School

Robb as a Peewee

older too, because I was almost always the youngest guy on my teams as I climbed the ladder of youth hockey. I was usually playing with kids a year or two older than me and I was prepared for that mentally because of my older brothers.

By the age of six I was already playing goalie as a mite. I don't remember why I initially gravitated towards the position, but that is where I wound up. I think I tried playing one game as a forward and after that I headed back to the crease to play goalie. I later skated out as a forward sometimes as well, to have fun and learn that aspect of the game, but for the most part I knew that I wanted to be a goalie. I loved playing in goal, there was just something about it that I can't describe. Maybe it was because nobody else wanted to play that position and I could claim it all my own, I don't know. I do know, however, that I was pretty good at it and that made me want to play there even more. I can recall, however, my mom trying to convince me to play another position. Like most moms she was worried that I was going to get hurt or something. I wanted to play goalie though and I eventually won out. I remember just loving the position and loving how much the goalie could impact the game.

In fact, some of my best memories of playing goalie as a little kid are recalling how good it felt to get patted on the back when I made a good save. I loved it when the guys would skate over and whack my leg pads with their sticks to let me know that I did good. That was all the reward I needed, I was hooked. The position isn't for everybody, that's for sure. But for me, it just clicked. I have loved it ever since. When you won the game and you were mauled by your teammates, that was just awesome. When they skate over to congratulate you and jump on you to celebrate, that is an emotion that's hard to describe. I remember another time when I was a kid and playing in the Twin Cities for a tournament. Well, we won our first game and later that night, back at the hotel, I was walking to the pool. Along the way my coach, Dale Atol, pulled me aside and told me how proud he was of me. He said I played a great game and just made me feel like I was on top of the world. Not surprisingly, we went on to win the tournament. Things like that really drove me to succeed and I still vividly remember that moment all these years later. That positive reinforcement drove me then and it drove me throughout my professional career too. The opposite effect was also true. I hated the feeling I got from when I knew I cost our team a win and that empty feeling drove me to be the best I could be.

Certain losses have really stuck with me over the years. I remember being a ten year old peewee and driving back up north to Duluth from the

"Silver Stick" tournament at the Bloomington Ice Garden. I felt responsible for the loss and when I got home that night I couldn't sleep a wink. I couldn't get over the fact that I felt that I had let my teammates down. I cried and cried, it was hard. I am pretty sure that if my mom and dad knew that I was in bed crying, as a ten year old, they would have probably had second thoughts on me playing goalie. But, I kept my emotions to myself and dealt with them on my own terms. Eventually I was able to figure it all out and that made me a lot stronger player both mentally and physically. Quitting was never an option for me, I would never stand for that. I just had to get better, and that is what I did. I realized that probably every goalie goes through those emotions at one time or another and that is what separates them from the other guys. Most kids can't hack that kind of pressure — especially at such a young age, but I was determined.

Before long my bantam team was playing in tournaments and traveling around Northern Minnesota. With all of my brothers playing on different teams, I don't know how my parents ever possibly managed to keep it all straight. They were just as dedicated as we were too, through thick or thin they got us to every practice and ever game. I remember one time going up to Thunder Bay during probably the worst blizzard I can ever remember. We drove up along Lake Superior and the lake-effect snow was so blinding. We had no business driving up there in those conditions, but mom didn't even think twice about it. We just loaded up and went, it was something I will never forget. My mom was driving and she just plowed along until we eventually got there. You couldn't see five feet in front of the car at times. We had to stop every so often just to make sure we were still on the road and not getting too close to the big cliffs along the side of the lake. I laugh about it now but it was so dangerous. We had a tournament to get to though and dangit, we were going to play hockey. Our parents were just as gung-ho as we were and as any hockey player will tell you, nothing can stop a hockey mom from getting her kid to a tournament.

That bantam team was pretty good. In fact, we won the bantam state title as well as the VFW title in 1980. I was 13 and that was my first taste of the big-time, I liked it a lot. I remember we beat Fergus Falls in both title games. Dale Atol was our coach and he was a great guy. My brother Pete played on that team too, which was really nice because I was the youngest kid on the squad. We had all been skating together since we were like six or seven years old and it was so cool to finally come together and just dominate the way that we did. Several kids from that team would go on to play Division One hockey.

Robb as a Bantam

Two years later, almost all of those same kids moved up the ladder to play on the varsity at Duluth Denfeld High School. I played on the junior varsity as a freshman and then started as a sophomore on the varsity in 1984. I will never forget, that year we came into the sectional finals undefeated but lost to St. Cloud Apollo, 3-2, at the State Fairgrounds Coliseum. It was my brother Pete's last game, which was really tough to see. I mean to get so close to making it to the tournament and come up short was the worst. I didn't play that great either, which made it even tougher. When that final buzzer sounded to end the game I was just devastated. I had been playing with that group of guys for so long and we were like family. I gave up a really bad goal at the end of that game, a soft wrist shot from way out, and took the loss personally. I will never forget staying on the bus in Forest Lake while everyone else went inside to eat at McDonald's. I just sat there and told myself that this was never going to happen again. I was devastated not only for myself, but also for my teammates. That drove me even harder.

That next year we lost quite a few seniors to graduation. In addition, our team's head coach, Bob Hill, left to serve as head coach at rival Duluth East so that he could be closer to his sons, Noel and Sean. (Sean would go on to play in the NHL for more than 15 years.) Hill was replaced by Bill Vukonich, who was a really good coach too. (Ironically, Vukonich's son would later go on to play at Harvard, the team which beat yours truly and the Gophers in the 1989 National Championship game in St. Paul.) Anyway, we had a great season that year but wound up losing to Coach Hill's Duluth East, Greyhounds in the playoffs.

We rebounded big-time in 1986 though, my senior year, to make it all the way to the state tournament. It was a team that wasn't as talented as the year before, but everything came together for us that season. We beat Duluth Central, 7-4, in section quarters, then Duluth East, 2-1, followed by St. Cloud

Robb in High School

Apollo, 6-2, and lastly Anoka in the section finals by that same score to finally make the Tourney. I will never forget this, but just prior to the championship game against Anoka, I sat down and wrote a letter to my teammates. I wanted to say something to truly inspire our team and remind them of just how far we had come. So, I thought about it and thought about it, and really laid it on the line. I poured my heart into that letter and told everybody that there was no way we were going to lose that game. I read the letter to the team before the team prayer and I don't think there was one guy in the room who wasn't crying. I teared up so quickly that I could barely read what I wrote, and I think that really moved everybody. I remember being on the ice for warm-ups, guys were coming up to me and asking me if I was OK. I was so emotionally lifted from that. Anyway, that game meant the world to me, and I wanted to make sure that my teammates were unified in our goal to win the championship. There was no way I wanted to experience the horrible feelings I felt two years earlier when we had come so close. This was my last chance to win it and I simply was not going to accept defeat.

Well, when we won the game that night and it was probably my greatest feeling in hockey ever. It was so special, it just meant the world to me. I will never forget the celebration with the guys afterwards out on the ice. It meant so much to West Duluth, to our fans, to my teammates and to my family. In fact, my brother Dan was so excited at that very moment that he actually leaped over the plexi-glass and flew onto the pile around the net — even beating some of my teammates to the celebration. I had told my teammates that we had a special bond, a chemistry, and we would never forget each other. That moment proved to be true. That was one of the most incredible experiences of my life.

With that, we headed south to the Cities to lace em' up. You know, making the tournament was all I ever wanted to do in hockey up to that point in my life. Like a lot of Minnesotans growing up, playing in the tourney was what it was all about. You start to watch it from the time you are six years old and to finally get there as a senior was very emotional. So, it was a dream come true for me, no question. I mean to play in the Civic Center in front of 18,000 fans, it was something I will never forget. It was a huge deal, my entire family was there. It made all the hard work, all the travel and all the sacrifices worth it.

My little brother Bill was also on that team and he actually got our first goal in the tournament quarterfinals against Bloomington Jefferson. We won that game, 4-2, but then lost to Burnsville, 3-1, in the semifinals. We went up 1-0 but they scored three unanswered goals from there to seal the deal. They had Scott Bloom on their roster, a future Gopher, and they were a talented team. That was tough. I was deflated by the loss but was more dis-

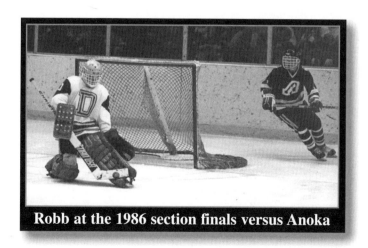

Robb at the 1986 section finals versus Anoka

appointed and sad knowing that it was all over. But, to be one of the last four teams standing at the end was special too. We wound up beating rival Hibbing to take third and that was a nice way to end it. Really, just to play in the tournament is the pinnacle of any young boy's hockey career and I was grateful to have experienced it first hand.

In retrospect, playing in the tournament really changed my life. Even though I had already been named to the All-Conference team, playing in the tourney and being on TV gave me some exposure that I wouldn't have otherwise received. You see, back then, in the mid-1980s, most colleges didn't start to recruit that hard until the end of the season. Plus, the University of Minnesota, the team I was dying to play for, already had their goalie situation pretty solidified by then. So, they didn't recruit me very hard at all. Coach Woog came to my house and offered me a partial scholarship and I took it. He was fair and he was honest with me. He told me that I wasn't going to play very much because they had a two-time All-American in John Blue coming back that next season. While I respected the fact that he was honest with me, the fact that he told me I wasn't going to play much was ultimately the deciding factor in my decision to accept the partial scholarship. Coming to college at the U of M was a real dream come true and I was thrilled. I love challenges and I knew that it was going to be a huge challenge. Colorado College had offered me a full ride, but I wanted to play at the U of M. I remember, I wanted to go out to Colorado Springs to go on a recruiting visit and miss a few days of school to have some fun, but my mom was on to me and killed that idea pretty quickly. She knew I wanted to be a Gopher.

Another big moment from that year came when I was drafted into the National Hockey League. Now, the draft back in my day was nothing like it is today with all the television coverage and the agents and so forth. Well, anyway, I was sitting at home one day and out of the blue I got a phone call from Rogie Vachon, the general manager of the Los Angeles Kings. What's funny is that I didn't even know the draft was going on that day! Anyway, he proceeded to tell me in his thick French Canadian accent that I had just been drafted by the Kings with the 107th overall selection of the sixth round. I was like, great, cool. So, me, being caught totally off-guard, says stupidly: "Well, that's great, but that's not a very big deal though... I mean this is a long way away, right?" So, now this guy is probably thinking, "Wow, we just blew our sixth round pick! This guy doesn't even have pro hockey on his radar screen." I mean in Canada, if you are taken when you are 18 it is the biggest thrill in the world, but for me, being just out of high school, I really wasn't even thinking about it. I just wanted to make the Gophers squad and play college hockey. Anyway, they sent me a package in the mail after that with a tee shirt and a jersey and some Kings stuff, and that was cool, but to tell you the truth I really didn't want to even think about that. I just wanted to prove to myself that I could play college hockey. Then if there was an opportunity to play professionally down the road, I would cross that path when I came to it.

After graduating from Denfeld High School in 1986, I came down to Minneapolis to begin the next chapter of my life at the U of M. I came in knowing that Coach Woog expected me to accept my role as the back-up with the understanding that I was going to learn as much as I could from a great veteran goaltender in front of me, and that is what I did. I probably played in a third of the games my freshman year and I learned a ton. John Blue would go on to play in the NHL, so it was great to get the experience of playing under him for a season. Coming to school at the U was great. I had so much fun playing with guys who I had looked up to for a long time and just learning the ropes along the way. I really matured as both a hockey player as well as a person there too. Juggling school and practice and games on the weekends was tough, so you had to be disciplined with your time. I went 13-5 that season and we made it all the way to the NCAA Finals in Detroit, where we wound up losing to Michigan State.

That year I also got invited to play in the World Junior Championships. This was something that I knew very little about to be totally honest, but I was excited for a new challenge. I remember, I was just 18, it was my first Christmas away from home, I was in Prague, Czechoslovakia, in a communist country, and I was just so excited to be there. Playing overseas was great and as it turned out, I wound up becoming just the second goalie ever in USA Hockey history, besides 1980 Olympian Jim Craig, to beat the Czechs and Russians in the same tournament. We wound up losing a medal to Sweden, but it was a great experience to be there and to play against that level of competition. I learned a very valuable lesson while playing there too. The other goalie, a kid named Pat Jablonski, had played at a pretty high level in the Canadian Major Junior system and was pretty well known. He had a track record with the other players and as a result, he was slated as the No. 1 goalie. Well, I remember one day in practice, a player from Michigan took a high shot at my head and I took offense to it. So, I went up to him right after that to say something to him and he said something like "what does it matter, you're nothing but

Robb as a Gopher

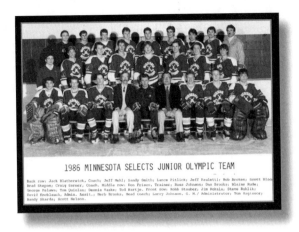

1986 MINNESOTA SELECTS JUNIOR OLYMPIC TEAM

Back row: Jack Blatherwick, Coach; Jeff Mehl; Sandy Smith; Lance Pitlick; Jeff Pauletti; Rob Broten; Scott Bloom; Brad Stepan; Craig Garner, Coach. Middle row: Don Frisov, Trainer; Russ Johnson; Dan Brooks; Blaine Rude; George Pelawa; Tom Quinlan; Dennis Vaske; Tod Hartje. Front row: Robb Stauber; Jim Rokala, Steve Rohlik; David Knoblauch, Admin. Assit.; Herb Brooks, Head Coach; Larry Johnson, G. M./ Administrator; Tom Ragischek; Randy Skarda; Scott Nelson.

a target for us out here anyways..." I was so furious and that was all the motivation I needed to succeed. I wasn't getting any respect from the players and that just drove me to play harder.

I knew that for whatever reason Jablonski wasn't that excited to be there and it showed in his performance. It's not that he wasn't a good goalie, or wasn't capable, it was just his attitude. I learned right then and there that your heart has to be in it. I was really excited to be there, where as Pat looked at it like it was just another stepping stone on the road to bigger and better things. He was supposed to be the starter there, but when the coaches saw my enthusiasm and hard work, they reversed our roles and made me the starter. It didn't take long for me to earn the respect of my teammates after that. That is a great lesson for young goalies: if you are going to play this position you have to realize that at times it will annihilate you if you are not totally 100% focused on why you are there and are not enjoying what you are doing. Attitude is everything in this game, and particularly at this position.

After my freshman year I remember trying out for the upcoming 1988 Olympic Team. There were some really good goaltenders trying out for the team and I knew it was going to be tough. Despite the fact that I played really, really well, they felt I was too young and went with Mike Richter, Chris Terrieri and John Blue — all of whom went on to star in the NHL. You know, I think sometimes things happen for a reason. Sometimes we think things are so bad, but sometimes they turn out to be a blessing — you just don't realize it at the time. As frustrating as it was being cut from the Olympic team, that drove me even harder and it all worked out for the best.

We (the Gophers) wound up going 34-10 that year and had an unbelievable season. What was amazing about it was that we lost a ton of guys to the NHL and Olympics that year; guys like Tom Chorske, Dave Snuggerud, Corey Millen, Todd Richards and John Blue. We weren't supposed to be very good that season but we came together as a team and surprised a lot of people, including ourselves. We won the WCHA title but came up short at the NCAA's Frozen Four yet again, this time losing a heart-breaker in the final 12 seconds to St. Lawrence out in Lake Placid, NY. It was the worst way to lose, but it was a great season nonetheless. The silver lining in it all was the fact that my big brother Pete's team, Lake Superior State, was able to win it all. That was really special to be there and to share that with him.

All in all, it was also one of the most fun seasons of hockey I have ever had. Guys just stepped it up a notch and we all played the role of underdog that year. Personally, it was almost like a fairytale. In fact, it was probably one of the greatest years of my life. With the help of my teammates I was honored as an All-American and became the first goalie ever to win the Hobey Baker Award, given annually to the top U.S. college hockey player. It is the Heisman Trophy of college hockey and I was extremely humbled and honored to win it. I was on top of the world at that point but I was hungrier than ever to get what my brother had just gotten, a national championship.

Playing for the Gophers was so much fun and living in the Twin Cities was like a whole new world for me. It was cool to be away from home, yet nice to be close enough to still see my family every now and then. In fact, my parents came down to most of my home games to watch us play. I will always remember going out to dinner with them at the Perkins over on Riverside Avenue afterwards. It was just a little tradition we did, but something that I still look back on so fondly. (In fact, one of the waiters is still there to this day and when I go back we always say hello and reminisce.) I remember one time after a really bad loss they were waiting for me after my game to go out to dinner. Well, I was so embarrassed by the way I played that I just did not want to go up those stairs at old Mariucci Arena to face them. I wanted to just crawl back to my dorm room and go to bed. My dad eventually saw me trying to escape, but instead of making excuses for me, he just hugged me. He didn't say a word and that was it.

Looking back, I was so lucky that I didn't have psychotic parents who yelled and screamed after my games on the car ride home. They truly "got it," and just loved me no matter what. They knew that I was my own harshest critic and that there was nothing that they could say that would make me feel any better or worse. So, they just loved me unconditionally and encouraged me to do my best. That was amazing and I now that I too "get it," I could never begin to thank them enough for being that way. They didn't care if I won or lost, they just wanted me to be happy and successful in life. They were proud of me for being the starting goalie on a Division One hockey team and they were proud of me for getting a scholarship. I think they were also proud of me for just being me. As long as I worked hard and did my best, both on and off the ice, then that was good enough for them. I was very lucky to have such great parents. They just kept it all in perspective and I was grateful for that.

Hometown Heroes...

THE HOBEY BAKER AWARD

Each April the nation's best collegiate hockey player receives the Hobey Baker Award, college hockey's equivalent to the Heisman Trophy. The recipient is the player who best exemplifies the qualities that Hobey Baker himself demonstrated as an athlete at Princeton University in the early 1900s. Baker was considered to be the ultimate sportsman who despised foul play — picking up only two penalties in his entire college hockey career. With his speed and superior stick handling, Baker opened up the game of hockey and set new standards for the way the game was played. A true gentleman, his habit of insisting upon visiting each opponent's locker room after every game to shake their hands became a model for today's players. An American hero, Baker gave his life as a decorated pilot in W.W.I. In 1981 Bloomington's Decathlon Club founded the Hobey Baker Memorial Award and each year the coveted honor is presented to the nation's top skater. The top hockey coaches, players, media and fans from around the country, as well as the finalists themselves, fly in to attend the gala event each year in Minneapolis. The balloting for the award is voted on by the nearly 50 NCAA D-I coaches who are asked to pick the top three players in their league as well as the top three in the nation.

PAST HOBEY WINNERS:

Year	Recipient	School
2005	Marty Sertich	Colorado College
2004	Junior Lessard	University of Minnesota-Duluth
2003	Peter Sejna	Colorado College
2002	Jordan Leopold	University of Minnesota
2001	Ryan Miller	Michigan State
2000	Mike Mottau	Boston College
1999	Jason Krog	New Hampshire
1998	Chris Drury	Boston University
1997	Brendan Morrison	University of Michigan
1996	Brian Bonin	University of Minnesota
1995	Brian Holzinger	Bowling Green University
1994	Chris Marinucci	University of Minnesota-Duluth
1993	Paul Kariya	University of Maine
1992	Scott Pellerin	University of Maine
1991	David Emma	Boston College
1990	Kip Miller	Michigan State University
1989	Lane MacDonald	Harvard University
1988	Robb Stauber	University of Minnesota
1987	Tony Hrkac	University of North Dakota
1986	Scott Fusco	Harvard University
1985	Bill Watson	University of Minnesota-Duluth
1984	Tom Kurvers	University of Minnesota-Duluth
1983	Mark Fusco	Harvard University
1982	George McPhee	Bowling Green University
1981	Neal Broten	University of Minnesota

In 1989, my junior season, we came as close as humanly possible to winning it all, and sadly, it happened right in my own backyard. We had another great season that year, going 34-11-3, and won another WCHA championship. Things looked promising for the team at the start of the season. Dave Snuggerud and Tom Chorske had returned from the Olympics and we had a bunch of quality players in guys like: Randy Skarda, Todd Richards, Lance Pitlick, Bret Strot, Luke Johnson, Jason Miller, Ken Gernander, Dean Williamson, Peter and Ben Hankinson, Larry Olimb, Grant Bischoff, Jon Anderson, David Espe, Tom Pederson and Travis Richards. We made it to the post-season and from there, we went on to beat rival Wisconsin in the NCAA

Robb with his Hobey

quarterfinals at Mariucci Arena to advance to the Frozen Four — which was being held right in St. Paul at the Civic Center. To be back at the Civic Center was very emotional for me. It was just four years earlier that I had come up short in the high school tournament and I did not want that to happen again.

Well, we beat Maine in the opener, 7-4, and that put us into the NCAA Finals against Harvard. I played OK in that game but hung in there thanks to all of our fans. I think they could sense that it was finally our time to win it all. It had been a decade since Herbie Brooks' Gophers had brought home the hardware and they were hungry for more. I could feel the excitement and was ready for the drop of the puck. Hockey in Minnesota is like religion and I did not want to let these people down. You could just feel the electricity in the air. It was such a big build-up and so much attention was on us.

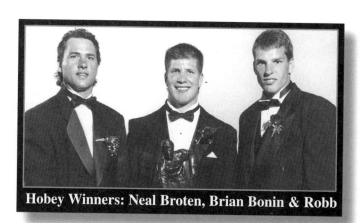

Hobey Winners: Neal Broten, Brian Bonin & Robb

We came out strong against Harvard on Jon Anderson's early goal to give us a 1-0 lead. I let in a pair of goals in the second period to Harvard's Ted Donato and Lane MacDonald, but we rebounded on Jason Miller's fourth goal in three games. The Crimson went ahead in the third on Donato's power-play goal, only to see Pete Hankinson tie it up at three apiece with a nice wrister. With that the buzzer sounded and we headed to overtime. As a goaltender you know that anything can happen in overtime. You pretty much know that you are either going to be the hero or the goat though, and that just adds to the pressure of it all.

Well, the extra session got underway with both teams skating hard. You could just feel the tension in the arena, it was unbelievable. A few minutes into it Kenny Gernander fed the puck to Randy Skarda, who then skated down the ice, made a move and took a slapper at Harvard Goalie Chuckie Hughes. It was like slow motion. Then, all you could hear was a "plunk," which could've only meant one thing: Skarda hit the pipe. We were crushed, but the game continued on. Then, at 4:16 of sudden-death, Harvard's Ed Krayer got a gift. They had gotten a lucky bounce off the boards which brought the puck back into our zone. I stopped the initial slap-shot but it got me out of position. Then, when I was scrambling back to get the rebound, Krayer scooped it up and slid a back-hander under my sprawled out pads to end the game, 4-3. I couldn't believe it. I just sat there motionless on the ice in utter disbelief. As I looked up, so too were the 19,000 Minnesota fans who couldn't believe what had just happened.

That was without a doubt one of the greatest college hockey games ever played. The atmosphere was electric, just so loud and unlike anything any of us had ever experienced before. There were so many things in that game I would've done differently. Sometimes in big pressure games you tend to be more reserved and play more conservatively than you'd like to.

Gopher Robb

Looking back I would have to say that it was by far the worst loss of my life. I will never forget that night for as long as I live. It was just devastating. I remember crying as I walked out of the Civic Center and just feeling so empty. I mean if Skarda's shot is one inch to the left we are national champs, but that is the way the puck bounces sometimes and we just wound up on the wrong end of that one. Hey, hats off to Harvard, they persevered and that is hockey.

All in all though, it was a great year and we had nothing to be ashamed of at all. We were so damn good. It was an amazing run and we just came up short. It was so heartbreaking to let down our fans like that. To send them home licking their wounds was very, very disappointing to say the least. You know,

Gopher hockey fans are so great, but when you are only 20 years old you don't realize that yet. But, as you get older, wiser and get to know more of those people, you realize just how special they are. They are just so passionate about their team and that is such a great thing. And they were so good to me, so good. It was the greatest experience of my life to play for the U of M and to play with so many great people. My only regret is that I wasn't able to give the fans a national title, and that will always stay with me.

Being a Gopher meant so much to and just to be mentioned alongside some of the legendary names which have passed through that program is so humbling. It's a great feeling to know that along the way I hopefully made contributions to the program that have had a positive impact. But I don't think I could ever impact the program the way the program has impacted me — that's for sure.

What made it even more sad for me was the fact that I knew that I had put on that Gopher sweater for the last time. I knew that I had not accomplished my ultimate goal of winning an NCAA title, but after three straight Frozen Four's I was ready to take the next step in my career in the NHL with the L.A. Kings. I thought about staying to resolve my unfinished business, but ultimately I decided to turn pro. Leaving school a year early was a tough decision but one I felt I had to make for myself. A lot of people don't know this but I even contemplated a couple of scenarios that would have allowed me to stay in school. I figured the L.A. Kings would wait and I could take one more shot at a title. I knew that the Frozen Four was going to be back in St. Paul two years later, so I thought about playing my senior year or even redshirting and coming back as a fifth year senior. That way I would have been in a great position to try again to win it all in our own backyard. I wanted to do that for not only myself and my teammates, but for the fans. I just wanted to give them that so badly. Well, in the end I went to L.A., but who knows what coulda, woulda, mighta happened had I stayed back. And, while I am sad that I didn't win an NCAA title, I have no regrets about my decision to play in the NHL. To have the opportunity to play at the pinnacle with the best players in the world is something every professional athlete strives for.

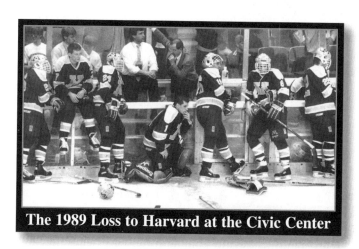

The 1989 Loss to Harvard at the Civic Center

CHAPTER THREE:
LIFE IN "THE SHOW"

With that, I signed with the Kings in the Summer of 1989. As I was soon going to find out though, it was going to be an extremely difficult transition from college to the pros. In college I had a coach and in the pros I had nobody, it was bizarre. I am not sure why it is that way, but that is the way it is. It was tough. I mean in college if I got into a slump my goalie coach, Paul Ostby, could pull me through it. But in the pros there was nobody there to lean on. Then, to make matters worse, I got hurt my rookie season and spent my first four months on the sidelines. Unfortunately for me, I had a lot of injury problems throughout my professional career and was actually hurt in eight of my 10 years as a pro. I remember though that when I was hurt I really focused on the mental side of the game. I mean I was at every Kings home game that first year when I was injured, watching the goaltenders, Kelly Hrudy and Mario Gosland, and learning from them. Then, I would visualize every play and try to make the same save in my mind, always focusing on getting better — even though I couldn't be out there skating at the time. Then, when I got healthy, I was ready to go and was mentally very sharp.

I remember coming right off the shelf and having two phenomenal weeks right out of the gates down in the minors. I was really surprised. I was hurt all that time and was instantly at the top of my game. In fact, I was playing so well that the Kings called me up. That was such an emotional thing, I will never forget it. I remember flying to meet the team in Winnipeg and then getting my first ever NHL start that next night against the Jets. The morning of the pre-game skate, however, I could sense that the speed of play was going to be an issue. Now, going from the minors to the majors is like night and day. The NHL is so much faster, it is not even close. Well, I got thrown to the wolves and unfortunately for me it was a terrible start to say the least. I got annihilated. I gave up two break-away goals like two minutes into the game and then let in another soft one shortly thereafter. Before you knew it we were down 3-0. They pulled me at the end of the first period and put in Ron Scott, who let in three more in the second period. So, they threw me back in for the third and I let in another three as we

Robb with the Kings

got hammered, nine to something. I was devastated. You go from playing in the minors, where you feel like you are on top of the world, to saying "Oh my God, what just happened here?!"

So, of course I started to question whether or not I was ready or whether or not I was even good enough to be there. I started to beat myself up pretty good. Then, two nights later I got the start in Calgary against the Flames and we got beat 5-2. I didn't play well that night either and I started to question my overall ability. I remember after that game, Rogie Vachon called me into his hotel room to tell me that the team had to set its playoff roster for the post-season. He sat me down and said he was sending me back down to the minors — the New Haven Nighthawks in the American Hockey League (AHL). He told me not to worry about the two games that I had played poorly in because they were going to send me down that next day and then immediately call me back up right away on what is called an "emergency recall." Well, funny, but it would take three long years before I would get that call! Maybe your phone wasn't working Rogie! I mean come on, it's like "Welcome to the National Hockey League kid, here's your cup of coffee... now go down to the minors for a few seasons." Unbelievable! That is just the reality of goaltending at that level though and there wasn't a thing I could do about it. They were down on me but they knew that the only thing that was going to help me was a lot of ice time. I was young and confused and didn't understand the business aspect of the game. But I vowed to work hard and stay focused so that I could get called back up as soon as possible.

My second year as a pro was even worse than my first. I got hurt in my very first game with New Haven after spending four months of my rookie season on the shelf. I tore the cartilage in my right knee in the season opener. It just popped. I was devastated. So, I had to decide right then and there what to do. Well, the decision was pretty easy. You, see, I was basically told that if I had surgery that I was going to be out for the entire season. So, I just sucked it up and played on it. Looking back it was a pretty stupid thing to do, but sometimes you just have to go with your gut. I had already missed one season and was not about to let an injury ruin my entire career. As a result, I spent all season in and out of the lineup, depending on how well I was feeling. The doctors told me that it was my decision and that it was up to me as to what I wanted to do. It was rough. I mean when you are not healthy it is tough to be at the top of your game, and that just made it even more difficult.

Finally, at the end of the year I had surgery. Here's what happened: You see, because the Kings' doctor was out of town, I had to see the Anaheim Angels' (baseball) team doctor instead. He told me that he didn't think that he was going to be able to save the cartilage in my knee but that I could expect a quick recovery from the surgery if it went as planned. Then, there was an alternate scenario whereupon if he felt that he could save the cartilage after all, he would do so. In that scenario it would have been a four to six month recovery. Now, this guy, not being familiar at all with the goalie position, made a critical mistake in not knowing the level of stress on the knees that a professional goaltender endures over his career. Anyway, when I woke up from surgery I realized that there was a cast on my leg which wasn't going to come off for at least two months. I was crushed. I knew that in addition to those two months that there was going to be several more just like it of hard core rehab. Meanwhile, in the recovery room I woke up to excruciating pain. As I was begging for pain killers, the nurses were trying to escort me out of there. I didn't even know how I was going to get home, let alone how I was going to just deal with the unbelievable pain in my knee. They then called me a cab, believe it or not, and basically propped me up on some crutches while showing me the door. I wound up at the Airport Sheraton Hotel, literally puking my guts out from the surgery, and realized that this is indeed a business.

The surgery was in April, now fast forward to August and I am back in Minnesota. I woke up one morning and my knee was as big as a softball. I immediately called my doctor and he referred me to a doctor at the University of Minnesota. I rushed in and the doctor told me that I had better see my specialist back in L.A. So, I flew out to see him and he proceeded to tell me that the surgery didn't work and that I was going to have to go under the knife all over again. By now I was getting used to life in the operating room, which was really sad. Five more months of rehab were now down the drain. Here I am, my third year as a pro and just about to enter training camp and my season is done yet again.

What was I going to do, quit? No way. I just dove in and started the long road back. After recovering from surgery, I even tried out for the 1992 U.S. Olympic team that December as a late addition, and trained with them for a few weeks. I was eventually released and spent the rest of the year splitting time between a pair of minor league affiliates in Phoenix and New Haven. I wound up finishing my third season in the minors and didn't know if I would ever get back to the NHL. Luckily, I had negotiated a five year "one-way" contract from the get-go with my agents Art Kaminsky and Jay Grossman, which allowed me to be paid as if I were playing in the NHL — versus the minor leagues. So financially I was OK — which was a huge relief.

As I now entered my fourth season of pro hockey, I finally caught a break. That Summer the Kings hired a new coach by the name of Barry Melrose. I didn't know who he was other than the fact that he had coached my brother Pete when he played in Adirondack, a minor league affiliate of the Detroit Red Wings. Now, for some strange reason, every time I had played against Adirondack, I played very well. So, that Summer I got a call out of the blue from Barry. He said, "Robb, I've seen you play, I know what you can do, now get ready to play 30 games this season with the Los Angeles Kings." That is how quick-

Robb During the Stanley Cup Run of 1993

ly your life can change in the National Hockey League. It was the break of a lifetime and it was so totally unexpected. I was just blown away. Barry had seen me play, believed in me and had confidence in me. For me that was huge, now I knew that I had an ally up at the top looking out for me. I had been going downhill for three years and this was just the break that I needed. Now it was up to me to work even harder to make the most of my opportunity.

I can still remember my very first preseason game that next year. It was against Vancouver and we got out-shot 55-20. I don't think the puck ever left our end of the ice, it was brutal. But, I hung in there and we wound up with a 3-3 tie. I played really well that night despite being bombarded. After the game Barry came up to me with a smile and said "Just like the minors, eh Robb?". He knew what I had been through, and for me that was all I needed to hear. I knew that at that point I was going to be on the roster and that things were going to be different. I knew that my coach had confidence in me and that was all it took, I was going to work really hard and try not to disappoint him. Two nights later I beat Pittsburgh and I just continued to play well throughout the preseason, going undefeated along the way.

Eventually, the guys began razzing me saying stuff like "So, this is the guy we have been waiting for the past four years..." It was awesome. You know, I had always been labeled as the "goalie of the future" and looking back I think that label is the kiss of death for any young player. I mean there is no future in hockey, it is who is hot right now and who can sustain it. That is all that matters at that level. You just have to prove yourself everyday. It is all about hard work and about "what have you done for me lately?". That is goaltending, plain and simple.

OK, fast-forward into the 1992-93 regular season, and I started out red hot. I was undefeated in my first 13 games, including the preseason, playing every third game behind All-Star Kelly Hrudy. Everything was working out great. My confidence was soaring and I was getting a lot of support from guys like Wayne Gretzky, who was really encouraging me whenever I was in there. My first loss of the season came on a penalty shot against Tampa Bay, which to no surprise occurred when I got caught out of the net in the corner and had to throw my stick in order to prevent a goal — which ultimately caused the game-winning penalty shot. Well, Barry still had a lot of confidence in me though and decided to play me in back-to-back games that next night. I played well for the rest of the season and definitely established the fact that I could play in the National Hockey League. So, looking back, Barry was the guy who took a chance on me and that is why I will always be indebted to him. He believed in me and gave me an opportunity and I will never forget that. What I did with that opportunity was up to me, but having that confidence allowed me to be my best and I made the most of it. Sure, we had our disagreements, but I had a lot of respect for him. As goaltenders we think sometimes that our coaches don't always make the right decisions, but that is usually water beneath the bridge. They are the coaches and they get paid to make tough decisions, regardless of what we may or may not think. Somewhere along the line we all need to catch a break, and for me, it was Barry Melrose who gave me that break.

Well, we wound up making the Stanley Cup Finals that season and that was something I will never forget. I had been playing more and more going into the playoffs and I just tried to keep that momentum going right into the post-season. I even got the start in our final regular season game, but got just hammered in a 6-0 loss to Vancouver. I was brutal, just terrible. We wound up playing Calgary in the first round, on the road. We had three goalies on our roster, and I didn't know if I would get the starting nod over Kelly Hrudy, but I certainly figured to be the back-up and get some starts along the way. Nope. Barry announced at a team meeting in his hotel room that night that Rick Nickel would be the No. 2. I was devastated. I went from thinking I had a decent chance to start, despite my horrific loss in the season finale, to basically getting benched. So, the meeting is over and everyone is walking out and I can't contain myself. I ran back into Barry's room and asked him what the deal was. Barry then asked me what my problem was. I got mad and said "What, I can't make your #$@*% lineup?". He screamed back, "You had your #$@*% chance, you were going to start these playoffs but you were just horrible that last game!" I agreed but couldn't believe he was going to bench me over one game. We were just going back and forth and it got really heated. We were nose to nose and neither of us was going to back down. I was so upset, I mean Barry had always preached about his reward system which basically rewarded players with playing time for hard work and dedication. I just felt completely let down. Anyway, I finally started to walk out of his room and as I was leaving I turned around and said one last thing: "By the way, your #$@*% reward system sucks!", and I slammed the door. I went back to my room and I didn't sleep a wink that night.

The next day in practice a lot of guys came up to me and told me to hang in there and I knew that they couldn't believe what Barry was doing. It was just a total slap in the face and my teammates knew it. Anyway, that night we got blitzed and the Flames scored something like nine goals on Kelly. It was brutal. We won the next night and things were suddenly all square. So, we head back to L.A. for Game Three and we wind up losing that one, which put is in the hole. The next day at our pregame skate before Game Four, Barry comes up to me and says very matter of factly: "Robb, you're starting in goal today." I was floored. I mean, I hadn't even dressed for the three previous games. I had been in street clothes sitting in the stands, and here I was back in goal just like that. This is the biggest game of the season, down two games to one, with our backs against the wall, and I get the call at home in front of our fans. After all that, telling him off, slamming the door and getting benched, here I am back in the starting lineup. Unbelievable!

It was a nationally televised playoff game on ABC that Saturday afternoon and I was just pumped. The place is packed and I look over and I see one of my biggest heroes, former President Ronald Reagan, sitting there ready to watch some hockey. I keep panning the crowd and then I see Kurt Russell, Goldie Hawn, John Candy, and a ton of other celebrities and I am just enjoying the moment — truly taking it all in. Then, we have this absolutely incredible National Anthem sung by this guy named Warren Weebie, who was such a great singer, and I am just jacked, knowing that my friends and family are all watching back home in Minnesota. The hair was literally standing up on the back of my neck and I was so ready to play. I just loved the pressure and knowing that I was going to be making an impact on the outcome of the game, good *or* bad.

Finally, they dropped the puck and just as I had hoped, I played one of the best games of my life and we won 2-1. Afterwards, I was interviewed on ABC and of course what do they want to talk about? Barry sitting me and then bringing me back in dramatic fashion — all by design of course. They made him out to be a genius and at that point I just smiled and nodded along. I finally said "Look, this is the toughest position and I don't ever want to get embarrassed. I always come prepared to play, and quite frankly I don't have to have somebody teach me a lesson to be prepared. I know that I didn't play well in our season finale, but I didn't need to go through all of that to get motivated to play hockey." Who'da thunk I had such a flare for drama? After that I knew that I had to just refocus on the remaining series ahead.

We then went back to Calgary, barely won Game Five and then returned to L.A. ahead just three games to two. I got the call again, and we won Game Six in a shoot-out, 9-6. It was a total turnaround and we went on to win the series. Winning that series remains one of the most memorable moments of my entire career. From there we played Vancouver in round two and I got the start in Game One. We were out-shot and despite playing well we lost. Barry called me in after the game and told me that he was going to start Kelly that next night but that he was very proud of me. He said my performance was exactly what we needed, but that he was going to give Kelly a shot in Game Two. He was very respectful and I was OK with that. Well, Kelly won Game Two and then got on a roll that was just amazing. He was just phenomenal from there on and we went on to win that series in six games. Then, we went to Toronto for the conference finals and we wound up beating the Leafs in seven games in one of the all-time classic series in NHL history. Gretzky would later say that that Game Seven was the best of his life. He scored three goals and assisted on another in a 5-4 win, it was awesome. What was so great about that was the fact that a prominent reporter from the Toronto newspaper had just written an article that morning about how Gretzky looked like he had a piano on his back for the entire series. That was all the motivation Wayne needed and he made them pay like he always did. Anyway, Kelly was on fire and I couldn't argue with Barry sticking with him. I just wanted to support him and be a team player. That is all you can do at that point.

Taking a Knee in L.A.

With that, we found ourselves headed to the Stanley Cup Finals to face off against Montreal. Now, as a goalie you want to play every game and it is tough to sit on the bench. But at that point I just wanted to get my name on the Stanley Cup and was willing to do whatever I had to in order to get it. Well, Kelly stands on his head and we wind up winning Game One up in Montreal. We are all totally pumped and we don't think anything can stop us at this point. Then, in Game Two, Marty McSorley gets called for having an illegal stick and we blow a 2-1 lead with under two minutes left. They scored on the ensuing power play right off the opening face off and you could just feel the momentum swinging the other way. They went on to win in overtime. OK, we head back to L.A. for Game Three and every celebrity on the planet is at the Forum to watch us. Gretzky has made hockey trendy in Southern California and everybody is on the bandwagon big time at this point. We thought we would rebound in front of our home crowd, but Montreal goalie Patrick Roy was unbelievable for the Canadians and we wound up losing both games at home in overtime. (Incidentally, Montreal set a record by winning 10 of their 16 Stanley Cup Playoff games in overtime that post-season.) We were all devastated. Then we wound up losing Game Five up in Montreal and it was over just like that.

It was a great ride though and definitely one of the greatest seasons of my life. I was also proud of the fact that I led the team that season in win percentage, saves percentage and goals-against average. Everything about that year was awesome, I will never forget it. Gretzky was awesome to play with too, just a great teammate. Wow, what a thrill. He was such a great guy on and off the ice. His work ethic every single practice was contagious, and his commitment to the game off the ice was just so impressive. He was a great role model for the young players, and even the more seasoned veterans looked up to him, not only because of his play on the ice, but for the way he conducted himself in the locker room and behind closed doors.

But in the end it was very painful to lose in the Finals like that. I wanted my name on Stanley's Cup so badly I could taste it. It was particularly frustrating for me because I thought that I was playing well at the time. As a goaltender, you never want to root against your partner or anything like that, and I was totally supportive of Kelly. I sincerely wanted him to play his best and was always ready just in case he got injured or got pulled. That is just the nature of the position and learning how to be unselfish and share time with your partner is all a part of the game. When one of you gets hot, the coach will stick with you until you cool down, and then he will go back to the other one, that is just how it is.

CHAPTER FOUR:
THE WRITING IS ON THE WALL

So, to put all that into perspective, it all comes down to believing in yourself and making the most of your opportunities. You have to believe in yourself and work hard. Period. I had always had a lot of confidence in myself, but I just needed somebody else to see that in me too and Barry was that guy for me. Sure, I have had my confrontations with certain coaches, but it was always well thought out. I tried to be a good listener and then very methodically and patiently figure out the best way to respond. Sometimes that meant being emotional, other times it meant being angry, but it was always well thought through and intelligent. I also tried to really pick my battles too. It is important to not go to the well too many times over issues that aren't critical to you. Then, when the major ones come, you can really bring out the big guns. I probably had at least a half dozen or so big-time blow-ups with coaches in my career, and they weren't always over the typical playing time issues. I mean you would be mad every other night if that were the case, so for me I picked and choosed which battles I really wanted to fight for and that way I had a better chance of winning. A lot of my arguments were over principle issues too, which is really the way that I am in everyday life. I can take a lot of heat, but there is a line for me and once that line is crossed... watch out. And hey, you don't always win em' either. In fact, that is probably why I got traded.

Here is how it all went down: It was the 1993-94 season, I had just come off of playing in 33 games during our Stanley Cup run with the Kings, and then that next season we didn't even make the playoffs. I wound up playing in only 22 games that year and a big part of that was because we got off to such a poor start. As a result, Barry kept going back to the veteran, Kelly Hrudy, whenever we got in trouble to bail us out. We were one of the worst teams in the league that year but I still had one of the top 10 best save percentages in the NHL. That was pretty hard to do on a team that struggled as much as we did, but I kept the same positive approach and made the most of my time in net. Barry was down on me that year and I think he was just down on everybody because we didn't play up to our ability. I guess I don't blame him, after all he was ultimately the one on the line for the team's performance.

That next year the Kings fired their general manager and brought in a new guy, Sam McMaster, who proceeded to draft an 18-year-old goalie by the name of Jamie Storr right out of the gates. The writing was on the wall right away with this guy. I mean you could bet the house that this guy was going to go with his first round pick no matter what and that did not bode well for me. You could see it a mile away, I was on my way out. Well, ironically, that was the year of the NHL lock-out and we ultimately didn't start playing until January. The Players Association had forewarned us that we could get locked out that season by the owners and that we should prepare ourselves financially for a work stoppage. None of us took it too seriously at that point though because we figured it would get settled before any games were missed. So, when it did finally happen we were all kind of in a state of shock. The union had advised us all to just go home and wait it out and to not get into any long-term financial deals just in case the thing dragged out for a long period of time. Well, I had just rented a house in Los Angeles by that time and was stuck out there. Since I couldn't make a living playing hockey, I decided to take up an offer a buddy of mine gave me to sell cars with him at a Toyota dealership out in an area of L.A. known as Little Saigon. Not knowing how long I was going to be out of work, I said "Sure, why not?".

I will never forget getting dressed up and showing up for my first day on the job. I met my buddy, who was the general manager of the dealership, and we went into his office for a crash course in how to sell a car. He says, "Robb, there are four ways to do a deal: cash, lease, financing or trade-in. Do you have any questions? No? Then you are ready to hit the sales floor my friend. Good luck, I will talk to you later." I just started laughing and said "Ready for what!" That was it, he took off and so concluded my formal training. So, I walk over to one of those little cubical offices along the side of the room to call my wife and tell her what was up. Just then this little guy comes over and says "Hey, that's my phone a-- hole, get the hell out of my office!" By then I am just laughing out loud wondering what on earth I am doing there. I mean just the other day I am being interviewed on ABC Sports and now I am getting kicked out of a cubicle by a guy wearing a clip-on tie. I just said the heck with it and tried to have some fun while I was out there waiting this thing out. When I stepped back and thought about it, it was pretty funny. I mean here I am, this 23 year old kid with an NHL contract, selling cars with these high pressure commission hounds. These guys were so competitive too. On slow nights I would have them competing against each other, racing and stuff like that, in their suits. It was a riot. One Saturday afternoon we had like 26 sales guys out on the floor and there was an UP-list, where guys rotated on taking walk-in customers. Well, I was next on the list and a customer walked onto the lot from the service department and I naturally went over to ask if I could help him purchase a new car. He said "No thanks, I am just here for service." So, I turned around and walked back into the dealership, putting my name back on the top of the list. Wouldn't you know, but the guy who was up next just happened to be the top producing salesman. He then starts yelling at me "You're down, you're down..." meaning I am at the bottom of the list. Now, I am not one to get mad too easily, but I knew that I had to stand up for myself in this shark tank. So, after a few choice words on my behalf, he backed down and I promptly resumed my position at the top of the list. I later found out through the grape vine that this guy was connected into the Vietnamese mafia. I guess it was probably not the smartest thing for me to do at the time!

Anyway, the lock-out finally got resolved and I was able to give my notice to the boss. Talk about a totally unique experience though. You know what? It actually turned out to be a blessing in disguise. Believe it or not, it really cleansed my head and got me focused when we finally did get back on the ice. It was the first time since I was a little kid that I had some time off from hockey to just relax and reflect. It made me appreciate so much what I had and how lucky I was to able to play hockey for a living. I never took things for granted after that, it was a pretty humbling experience for me. In retrospect, I was glad that I took the job. Hey, I even sold eight cars — mostly to people who wanted my autograph I think, but who cares! The dealership had advertised the fact that I was working there during the lock-out as some sort of ingenious marketing ploy. They even had business cards made up for me that read *"Blue Line Stauber,"* the nickname that ESPN radio host Jim Rome had given me in reference to the fact that I loved to skate out of my crease with the puck. When it was all said and done I was glad to get my skates back on and return to my real job between the pipes. I learned a lot from that experience though, especially the fact that I really suck as a car salesman!

OK, the season resumes and it is the second game of the year. A guy skates in on me and fires a wicked slap shot. Crack! I break a finger on my stick hand. I can obviously tell that my hand is hurting, so I skate over to our bench at the next whistle. There, I showed our trainer my finger, which was bleeding profusely and pointing back at me all twisted around. The trainer then proceeded to take a band-aid and put it on the cut. Are you kidding me? I just skated back to my crease and sucked it up, knowing that it was for sure broken. So, here I am with yet another injury. The doctor told me it was a bad break and that I was going to have to be out for four to six weeks. Now, I knew that this new GM was looking for an excuse to get rid of me, but I wasn't about to give him the satisfaction. So, even though I was not cleared by our team doctor to face shots, I made sure not to miss any practices. During that time I did every skating drill with the team, even though I was injured. Finally, six weeks later I got cleared to play in games by the team doctor. I was so psyched to get back into the crease after yet another long layoff. We are on our way out to New Jersey for a series with the Devils and after practice that day I see that I am not on the list to make the trip out there. I am just livid. I went and put some clothes on, didn't even shower, and ran up to the GM's office. I am basically in underwear at this point, all sweaty, walking through the L.A. Lakers offices (The Kings and Lakers both played at the Forum Arena) on my way to see Sam and Barry. Well, I get there, and I am just steaming.

"What do you want to talk about Robb," says Sam. Are you kidding me? What do you want to talk about? How about why I am not making this road trip even though I am cleared to play" "Well, we want to send you down to get some more rehab time because of all the practices you have missed." What? I haven't missed a single practice. What about the other player, Troy Crowder? He is making the trip and he's missed a bunch of practices during that same time. "That's the way it is going to be," he said. So, I said no way, I am not going to the minors. You are not going to bury me down there, no way. You can trade me, but I am not going to be sent down. Barry jumps in at that point and says "No, no, Robb, that is not what we want…" I told him that I went to the minors that last season when I was injured and they sat me in the stands. Why would I want do that to myself again? So, they caved in and brought me on the road trip.

Just when I thought everything was starting to work itself out, three days later, on February 14, 1995, I got traded to Buffalo. The deal had me, Alexei Zhitnik and Charlie Huddey all going to the Sabres in exchange for Goalie Grant Fuhr, Philippe Boucher and Denis Tsygurov. It was a terrible trade for the Kings and everybody knew it. In fact, a lot of people in the media even said that it was one of the worst in franchise history. Hey, I stood up for myself though and ultimately came out in good shape. I did not want to be lied to. If he would have come out and told me that he was going in a different direction with a new goalie, I could respect that. But to accuse me of not trying hard and not practicing over a minor injury — that was insulting and I wasn't going to take it. The bottom line was that guy was just trying to justify his existence as an NHL general manager. He even wound up earning the nickname *"McMaster the Disaster"* because of all the poor deals he made. And by the way, his boy Jamie Storr, who he rushed into a position that he clearly wasn't ready for, has never been a starter in the National Hockey League.

I was sad to leave L.A. and I was sad to say goodbye to Barry. Barry challenged me to be my best and taught me so much about the game of hockey. I remember once when he approached me after a bad game and he just chewed my ass. He told me that sometimes I took it easy on myself and that I didn't challenge myself every night. At first I was mad, and then I thought about it and agreed. He made me look at myself to get better, and from that moment on I did challenge myself every night, no matter what. So, he confronted me on things like that and I appreciated it. He also taught me a lot about the media and that if you were willing to read the sports page when things were going good, you had better be willing to read it when things were going bad. He even taught me to take what the reporters said about you with a grain of salt. I learned a lot from Barry and have a lot of respect for him as a coach and as a person. Even though we didn't always see eye to eye, I always knew that he had my back. As I was about to find out over the next several years, that is a pretty valuable commodity in the NHL.

When I got traded to Buffalo I was really happy. Buffalo is a lot like Duluth, it is a smaller city and pretty blue collar. It had a real small town feel and coming from Los Angeles, I was looking forward to that different type of atmosphere. And, even though I loved playing in L.A., I was excited to be going somewhere new and to be getting a fresh start. I understood the business aspect of the game and I knew that I was probably going to bounce around over my career to several teams. That is just the nature of the business and particularly the nature of the position I play.

Coming to Buffalo I knew my role was going to be as a back-up. I mean after all, the starter there was none other than Dominic Hasek, arguably the greatest goaltender in the history of hockey. Anyway, I had no illusions about what my job was — there wasn't going to be a competition between us, that was for sure. I knew that I was going to learn a lot from being around him though and that I would get some decent ice time when he needed to rest. So, coming in it seemed like a pretty good situation for me.

I remember coming in to town in 1995 and feeling really good about my new opportunity. It felt good to be coming somewhere where I was wanted. I mean, they traded for me, right? So, that must have meant that they wanted me, right? Well, as I was about to find out, that is not always the way things work out. As I was about to learn, sometimes a coach can make your life a living hell for no apparent reason at all.

Now, the "Dominator" had truly earned his nickname, he really did. That guy was so dominant, just unbelievable. I was in awe of him when I saw him play. I can remember when I got there and I saw him play for the first time up close and personal, I couldn't believe the things he could do out on the ice. Well, as luck would have it, Dominic got hurt just before the playoffs and they wanted to rest him for a few weeks to make sure he was healthy. So, I was going to play in about a half a dozen games, which was great.

I just told myself that I wasn't going to be Dominic Hasek, I was going to be Robb Stauber. I was going to play my game and do the things that got me this far. If I did that then I knew I would do well. I was determined to play my game and let the chips fall where they may from there. If that wasn't good enough, than so be it, but that was my attitude going in.

OK, it's just after my first game with the Sabres and the head coach, John Muckler, takes me aside and tells me that he doesn't like the way I play the position. He tells me that he doesn't want me to skate out of my crease to stickhandle the puck and instead I need to focus on staying home. He was just a very old fashioned, old-school coach and he hated my style. He was exactly the opposite of my old coach in L.A., Barry Melrose, who encouraged me to just be myself. Barry knew that if I played "my game," then I would be successful. He understood that the way I would play my best was for me to play the way I was most comfortable out there.

Muckler, meanwhile, wanted to change me and my entire style 15 minutes after I stepped foot in the lockerroom. It was unbelievable. I mean why the heck did he trade for me? Muckler wasn't only the coach, he was also the general manager. So, it was his decision to bring me there and now he wants to completely change the way I play the game. Clearly, he knew the type of player that I was, right? For the life of me I couldn't figure this guy out and I was beside myself I was so upset.

Anyway, I played in my first game and I came out of the net, like I always did, and I could see Muckler just going crazy on the bench. Well, after the game he yells at me for coming out of the net to play the puck and is really upset. I didn't know what to do, I mean that is the way I instinctually play the game. I was so bummed out. Here I am in a new situation and already the coach is completely down on me. It was real-

Robb with the Sabres

ly tough.

The next day at practice we get ready to begin and Muckler blows his whistle to tell everybody to do a certain drill called a "dump-in," where the coaches have the pucks out at the red line and they ring them around the boards into the zone to simulate a play. The players then skate in and play the dump-in behind the net to start the break-out the other way. Well, at that moment I knew it was a set-up and that I was going to get nailed. I could see it as plain as day. He was testing me and wanted to bust me right there in front of everybody. He knew that my style of play was to go out and grab the puck to lead the break-out, rather than just sit in the crease and let the other team forecheck in to try and steal it away. That is the way I have always played the game and I wasn't about to change my entire philosophy for this guy.

Sure enough, the puck comes in and I head over to stop it before it goes around the boards, and I play it out to my defensemen who are starting the break-out. Well, as soon as I touch the puck Muckler blows his whistle and starts screaming and yelling at me right there in front of the entire team. He is shouting "You stay in that damn net..." and "Don't come out of that damn crease...". It was pretty embarrassing because I didn't even know most of my teammates at that point and here I am getting totally undressed by this guy in front of everybody. It was just awful.

My defensemen, meanwhile, know the type of goalie that I am and they totally prefer that style. They like goalies who can stickhandle and get them the puck so that they don't have to grind into the corners and get hit. They realized that a goalie who could do what I did was like having a sixth player out there, and that is a really valuable commodity at this level. I was stuck at that point. I mean here is this old-school coach who has this ancient philosophy on goaltending and wasn't about to get shown up. I knew that I was going to lose that battle every time.

Well, I hung in there and played a few more games, trying to do what he wanted. It took a lot of discipline, but I was able to change and adapt to please this guy — even though I absolutely hated it and felt 100% that it was wrong. Anyway, it is the last game of the season and Dominic is out, they are resting him for the playoffs. We are playing at home in Buffalo against New Jersey, who is really tough and actually goes on to win the Stanley Cup that year, in 1995. We are just about to go onto the ice to start the game and as we are leaving the locker room Muckler singles me out and says "Stauber, don't touch the @#$%& puck tonight!" I was done for. This guy hated me and there wasn't a thing I could do about it.

Sure enough, three minutes into the game a puck comes trickling down the ice just to the right of my crease. A Devil forward is chasing my defenseman back towards the puck and it is the perfect opportunity for me to go out and do what I always do: be aggressive and clear the puck out of the zone so that there wouldn't be any chance of the puck winding up in the back of my net. Well, Muckler is so in my head at this point that I don't really know what to do. So, I skate out, thinking way too much about what I am doing, hesitate, and then head back to the crease. I am now stuck in no-man's land without a clue and realize that I am dead in the water. The puck comes to me, I stickhandle it like a peewee and just fumble it. The forward grabs the puck and shoots it off my skates into a wide open net, 1-0. I am just sitting there with the red light flashing behind me thinking "You have got to be kidding me."

Psychologically, I am now toast. Within five minutes the score is 3-0 and they can smell blood. I am just a mess at this point, totally out of it. I didn't know what to do, I was just awful. Muckler's comments were all I could think about and I was having a complete meltdown. Anyway, I survived the first period and am in the locker room trying to get a grip. I am sitting there with my face down and a towel draped over my head, just like in the painting on the cover of the book. So, I dug deep and tried to muster every positive thing I could think of to get my head in the game. I vowed to play my way and forget about what he told me. I did not want to let down my teammates and I did not want to lose the game, so I threw caution to the wind and headed back out there on my own terms.

Incredibly, I played awesome from there on out. We tied the game and went up 5-3 late in the third period. New Jersey then pulls their goalie, Marty Brodeur, and they attack with six skaters and an empty net. I wound up letting in one more goal after that with just a few second left, but we still hung on to win 5-4. I was so pumped, just totally proud of myself. My teammates were so psyched for me because they knew what was going on. They knew what I was going through and were coming up to me afterwards to congratulate me on an incredible comeback.

When I was getting undressed our team leader, Wayne Pressley, came over to me, looked at me and said "That was unbelievable..." He knew that I had pulled off something pretty amazing that night, to go from playing so horribly in the first period to getting a win was very special. His comment to me made me feel so respected and I will never forget that. Then, one of the assistant coaches, John Tortorella, comes over and says "That's a professional, a true professional...". That meant the world to me too, it felt great.

Shortly after that the goalie coach, Mitch Korn, one of Muckler's hires, comes over and just starts laying into me about everything I did wrong that night. He is just going off and I am like "You have got to be kidding me!". I am on cloud nine at this point and then this guy comes over and just lays into me. One of the other players actually came over at that point and told Korn to get out of my face and to just back off. The guys knew what I was going through and weren't about to let this guy bring me down after that. Korn never played at this level and he had no idea about how the mental battles can effect you. None. He understood the fundamentals and that was about it, so I just tuned him out and tried to enjoy the moment. (Incredibly, that moment effected me so profoundly that it impacted the way I coach to this very day.)

Well, we wound up losing to Philly in the first round of the playoffs that year and it didn't take a rocket scientist to figure out where I was headed. I knew that the writing was on the wall yet again for me and knew that I was going to be sent down to the minors that next season. So, I went in for my year-end exit-meeting with the coaching staff, to evaluate my performance and discuss the future. Muckler and I started talking and I just told him that it was really tough for me to change my style that late in my career. I told him that even if he didn't like my style that I was going to give it 100% and compete as hard as I possibly could. I knew that Dominic was the starter and that was OK with me, I just wanted to be a part of the team and to do my job even if that meant being a back-up.

The bottom line here is that Muckler traded for me and then suddenly came down with a bad case of buyer's remorse. I was just doomed from day one with that guy. So, that Summer Muckler went out and traded for another goalie, Andrei Trefilov, and I knew I would never see the ice in Buffalo ever again. I reported to training camp that Fall though and played great, literally giving up one goal in all of my games that I played in. It was one of the best training camps of my career.

Sure enough though, Muckler called me into his office and told me that he was sending me down to the minors. I wanted to stay positive so I told him that I was going to try my hardest down in Rochester, NY, their minor league affiliate, and that I was going to work on getting better everyday. Then, as I was about to walk out of his office, I paused, looked right at him, pointed my finger at him and said "John, I am not going to let you tell me that I can't play this game..." Then I just walked out. That was it.

From there I just tried to make the best of it. And do you know what? I was having fun. I started out strong and was really playing well. Then, believe it or not, Muckler rears his ugly head yet again. The guy just couldn't leave well enough alone. Get this. I am playing in Rochester which is about 60 miles from Buffalo. Well, there is a clause in every NHL player's contract, which was a part of the collective bargaining agreement (CBA), that says if you are ever sent down and it is more than 40 miles away from the parent club, then they have to pay for your housing.

Meanwhile, I had already bought a house in Buffalo, figuring I was going to be there for a while. So, I submit my expense report detailing the cost of my house payment in Buffalo, figuring that I would pick up the cost of my apartment in Rochester on my own. I mean there was no way I was going to drive through traffic an hour and a half each way from Rochester to Buffalo every day, so I got a cheap apartment to stay in while I was there. It was all legit, spelled out as clear as day in the CBA.

When Muckler caught wind of that he flipped. He had the assistant GM call and threaten me and basically read me the riot act. I was totally floored. I couldn't believe how far this guy was trying to bury me. He took such a personal vendetta against me and to this day I have no idea why. Well, I wasn't about to roll over on this. A) it was a lot of money and B) it was the principle of the whole thing. Pretty soon I realized that nothing was getting paid and that they were stiffing me on it. So, I had to get my agent involved and we had to jump through all of these legal hoops, which was totally ridiculous.

I mean I am making close to a half million dollars a year at this point, but there was no way I was going to back down over a $2,500 monthly house payment. I was entitled to it and I was not going to let Muckler do this to me, no way. It got so ugly I couldn't believe it. I had to practically beg these guys to read the rules and accept the fact that they were wrong. Hey, my career was on the line. I did not want to drive an hour and a half twice a day, sometimes two or three times a day depending on training and meetings. I needed to be fresh not only for me but also for my team's success. I needed to be sleeping in Rochester, not Buffalo.

Just when I thought it couldn't get any more bizarre, one night during the season I got a call from Muckler and he just went off on me. He is dropping F-bombs left and right and screaming at me that I am not going to ruin his team. I very calmly told him that I was not on his team, I was on the Rochester Americans team. He then starts complaining about the CBA and what a joke it is. You see, this is all happening just after the NHL lock-out, so management and the players were still at odds with one another. I apparently was on the front lines of it all — unbeknownced to me.

Finally, they gave in and paid me the housing allowance that I was owed. It was like pulling teeth, but it eventually got done. Ironically, I was having one of the best seasons of my career that year until I blew out my shoulder midway through the season and had to spend the rest of the season on the shelf. Such is life in pro hockey.

The highlight of the season, however, came on October 9, 1995, when I fulfilled a lifelong fantasy by scoring my first goal ever. It was at the end of the game when they had pulled their goalie to try to tie it up. A guy shot the puck, I grabbed it and immediately dropped it so I could shoot it the length of the ice. It went straight in and my teammates went absolutely nuts. It was even the "Play of the Day" on ESPN's Sports Center! That was something I will never forget for as long as I live.

The next year I was a free agent and I got the heck out of there, signing with the Washington Capitals. Muckler was a cancer to me and I was thrilled to have him out of my life once and for all. So, I had a great season with Washington's minor league affiliate, the Portland Pirates. I made the AHL All-Star team and played really well. I even got called up for a while when Olaf Kolzig got sick, which was great to be back with the big boys.

The next year I rolled the dice and signed a free agent contract with the New York Rangers. I was feeling really good heading into training camp that Fall and was anxious to get out of the AHL and back to the NHL for good. I had a great camp with them and felt very good about my chances of landing the role of back-up to New York's All-Star goalie, Mike Richter.

Well, I didn't get the job but wound up heading down to their minor league affiliate in Hartford. Again, I could only control the things that were in my power, and that was it. So, I tried my best down there and played probably the best I have ever played in my entire career. The Rangers noticed too, and their GM and coach, Colin Campbell and Don Maloney, took a real interest in me. I was psyched because at this point I knew that there was a really good chance that I was going to get called up.

Flash forward to February, right before the 1998 Winter Olympics, in Nagano, Japan, and Colin Campbell calls my head coach of the minor league team I was playing on in Hartford. Richter was going to play for Team USA and was going to be gone for several weeks. With that, I got the green light to join the team in New York. It was the call I had been waiting for and I was so pumped. It was going to be my big break and there was no way I was going to screw it up. I was injury-free, I was playing great and I was hungry to show that I could play in the greatest league in the world.

So, I pack my bags and am about to head to New York. I meet with the P.R. guy at Hartford one last time and just before I am out the door he says to me "Hey did you hear the news? Colin Campbell got fired and his replacement is John Muckler." I stopped dead in my tracks and just started laughing. If I could have cried at that moment I probably would have done that instead, but I was too out of it to even comprehend what I was doing. I simply couldn't believe my ears.

Not knowing what to think, I drove to New York and suited up to practice with the Rangers. I was excited to be back in the "show" and wanted to make the most of it. Sure enough though, it was the first day of practice and lone behold, there was Muckler. I just ignored him and hit the ice. I had a great practice and felt confident. Then, after practice I am getting dressed and just as I had suspected, I get the word that I am being sent packing back to Hartford. Unbelievable! I just spent two and a half years in the minors battling injuries and bad luck and now, here I am with a golden opportunity that just gets crushed. Muckler showed me up in Buffalo and now he showed me up again in New York. Talk about bad luck.

So, I went back to Hartford and played great, finishing second in the AHL in almost ever statistical category and was again named as an AHL All-Star. Believe it or not, Muckler told the Rangers GM, Don Maloney, that despite my efforts, he wanted to get rid of me once and for all. He wanted to sabotage me and was bound and determined to do so. Incredibly, Maloney overrode him and offered me a contract. I was blown away. I also wasn't stupid. There was no way I was ever going to play with him behind the bench.

With that, I politely declined the offer. I told Don that I thought they hired the wrong coach and to mark my words, he was going to regret his decision to hire John Muckler — sooner than later. It was a ballsy thing to say, but I had to get that off my chest. I knew that Muckler hated me and for me to stay it would have been career suicide. It was tough though, because I really enjoyed playing in Hartford. I just felt that I had worked too hard to get hammered by this vindictive guy, so I signed with Winnipeg in the International Hockey League (IHL).

Looking back, this was the biggest mistake I ever made in my career. The AHL was where all the young talent was; guys heading up the ladder. The IHL, meanwhile, had more of the older players; guys who were on their way down. For whatever the reason, I flat-out made a poor decision. As a result, I didn't have much fun playing there, which meant I didn't play very well either. After about one month up in Manitoba I decided that I needed to be proactive and really try to resurrect my career. I was 29 years old and desperately wanted to be back in the NHL. I knew that I could play at that level and was not about to get stuck in the minors forever. I was dying on the vine and needed to escape in a hurry.

So, I called my old roommate from when I played in Los Angeles, Dave Taylor, who was now the King's GM. I knew that they had suffered some injuries and were in desperate need a goalie. I figured this was going to be my last shot and went after it hard. I got my agent on the horn and the ball started rolling really quickly. I was so excited. By now I was desperate to get out of the IHL and was hoping so much that this was going to somehow work out. I begged Dave to just give me a chance and promised not to let him down. I wanted to play in the NHL so badly at this point that I could taste it.

He asked me about my injuries, which is what hurt me so badly when we were teammates together. I explained to him how I had been injury free for two years and that I was in top shape. I was ready to go and just needed an opportunity. He said he would give it some thought and get back to me. Well, the next night I am playing in Chicago and after the game I saw on the news that L.A. had just signed Ryan Bach. He was a rookie goalie who had never even played in the NHL and was a marginal minor league player at best. I was absolutely crushed. Then, I remember watching him play for the Kings on ESPN that very next night, it was just torture. He let up a bunch of soft goals early and got yanked right away too, which made it even worse for me to stomach.

It was like somebody had just stabbed me in the back, I was devastated. Looking back I realized that I was probably a day late in calling Dave. They had already been negotiating with this guy when I called and I think it was a done deal even before I entered the picture. Again, just bad timing and bad luck. Who knows? If I had gotten a hold of Dave maybe a day or two earlier, I think it would have been a no-brainer. I would have been back up in the NHL and my career would have gone an entirely different direction.

In the meantime I am now totally deflated. The wind is out of my sails and I am completely depressed. I figured that if I couldn't even convince my old roommate to give me a shot, then I must be all washed-up. That was all I needed to push me over the edge. I played one more game for the Manitoba Moose, sucked completely, and then called it a career. It was over just like that. It was no longer fun and my heart was no longer it in at that point. I wanted no part of that, so I packed up and moved home to Minnesota. Looking back, I am glad that I was able to leave the game on my own terms. Luckily, I didn't suffer a career ending injury that would've messed me up later in life or anything like that either. I see players who went through that and can't play with their kids now, and I never wanted to go through that. Sure, it wasn't the ideal way I wanted to retire, but it was on my own terms. The game wasn't fun anymore and for me that is when I knew that I needed to get out and pursue my other dreams, like getting into coaching. Hey, I could have stuck around for five, six or seven more years in the minors making a hundred grand a year, but it would have been nothing more than a job for me and that wasn't why I played the game.

If I didn't love it and I knew that I didn't have a shot to climb the ladder, I wasn't going to play very well. I needed to be challenged, that is what motivated me. Without that, I was just taking a roster spot that a younger guy on his way up deserved more than me. I still loved the competition, the team aspect of the game, and the guys, but my heart wasn't into it. I wasn't enjoying myself and figured I was ready to hang em' up. At a certain point hockey becomes all business and at that point it has to be treated as such.

The bottom line in this entire story is this: sometimes you get dealt a really bad hand and you just have to suck it up and make the best of it. If you play this game long enough there is a good chance that you will run across a coach or administrator who doesn't like you or your style and wants to change you. How you deal with that adversity is up to you. You just have to remember that there are consequences for everything you do, but ultimately you have to do what is best for you and for your career.

Sometimes things work out in your favor and sometimes they don't. Hockey and goaltending are not a perfect world. And do you know what? That is life. You have to be able to deal with it and just persevere. That is the key to success in this game. If you can do that, then you will be OK. Hey, I have no regrets, it was a great career and I was very lucky to have been able to make a living for as long as I did doing what I loved to do. I was ready to move on and that is exactly what I did. I wanted to come home to spend more time with my family and try some new business ventures. It was going to be a new beginning and I was excited about my future.

STAUBER BROTHERS SPORTING GOODS

In April of 1990, Stauber Brothers Team Choice Sporting Goods opened for business at Burning Tree Plaza in Duluth, Minn. The owners are the six hockey-playing sons' of Delano and Jean Stauber: John, James, Dan, Pete, Robb and Bill. The Original sporting goods store was a dealership called Team Choice and supported customers in several major sporting goods category lines which included hockey, softball, baseball, football and soccer. By 1993 Corporate Team Choice went out of business but the brothers maintained their clientele and renamed their business Stauber Brothers Sporting Goods. In early 1995, the brothers constructed their current building located at 2541 Maple Grove Road in Duluth, and relocated the business there in December of that same year. Today, Stauber Brothers Sporting Goods is a leader in the sale of athletic sporting goods and is well recognized throughout the states of Minnesota and Wisconsin.

"Opening the store was a really fun venture," said Robb. "I was mostly involved in helping to finance it but I also worked there a little bit too. It was fun to do something in my hometown and to be able to go into business with my five brothers. It is a grinding retail business though and very competitive too. While Jamie is the most involved with the day-to-day operations, none of the five brothers work there full-time. But, as they get older and retire from their 'real jobs' down the road, I am sure that they will probably focus more attention to it."

To learn more about the Northland's top hockey shop, check out the store near the Miller Hill Mall in Duluth. You can also reach them at (218) 727-3018 or visit their website at www.stauberbrothers.com.

CHAPTER FIVE:
THE END OF ONE DREAM &
THE GENESIS OF ANOTHER

When I retired from pro hockey I was anxious to relax a little bit and also try some new endeavors. In fact, back in 1993 Paul Ostby, my former goalie coach with the Gophers, and I began doing goalie camps together. Now that I finally had the time to really dedicate myself to teaching, I began researching the Summer camp scene much closer than I ever had. After studying the industry and seeing the obvious flaws, a light bulb went off in my head that would forever change my life, and more importantly, the lives of young goaltenders wanting to obtain elite level training on a year round basis. And so was born the idea for the Goalcrease.

The Goalcrease was conceived because I was so disappointed with the results of the one week camp system of teaching. I wanted to teach kids on a consistent basis, because goaltending is not like other positions, it requires more time and more specialized training. So, the genesis and inspiration of the Goalcrease actually came about as a result of pure frustration. I wanted to do something drastically different and really make a difference. It was a leap of faith and luckily it has turned into a real dream come true for me.

Basically, I wanted to help young goalies in the area get better and to give back to the community I came from. Well, after seeing what was out there over the years in terms of options for goaltenders, I knew that that wasn't the answer. For several years I would see the same kids coming back year after year to my camps with the same problems. They weren't really getting better, they were just going through the motions. It was really discouraging. I wasn't in a position to make a big impact on these kids' lives back then and that really motivated me to take a look in the mirror and do something. It wasn't that the week-long camps weren't good camps or that the people working there weren't good instructors. It was merely the fact that goalies were not the focus of the operation. They weren't getting the proper amount of time required to master new moves and that sort of thing. Goalies require more time to learn new things and it just wasn't feasible in that type of environment.

Realizing that there were very few options for goaltenders at the time, other than just attending general goalie camps, I knew that we couldn't keep running around the Twin Cities working with kids sporadically here and there at different arenas, it just wasn't having the type of impact that we wanted. From there, I had the vision of opening my own academy and doing everything I wanted to do on my own terms, just for goalies.

My thoughts were to develop a facility in the Twin Cities where the goalies would come to us. This wasn't going to be the typical summer camp which is all that existed prior to that. This was going to be a year round facility just for goalies, which would be staffed with nothing but goalies. This was to be our goalie heaven. It was also going to be a big financial risk, no question. Nobody had ever done this before and we were definitely getting into uncharted waters. I felt confident about our concept though and was willing to invest into the future of goaltending. I just knew deep down that it was going to work and that I would be doing something that would be making a difference. I have always felt that goalies are the most neglected athletes in any sport, yet they face maybe the most amount of pressure of any athlete in any sport. I mean to have the most pressure-packed position combined with the least amount of coaching — it just didn't make any sense to me. In the end I just felt like it was something that was desperately needed here and I believed in it. Plus, they needed a place where they could call home.

From there, everything started falling into place. We originally started the process of putting together a business plan and meeting with the banks in the Spring of 2002. We then began looking for commercial real estate around the Twin Cities and finally secured what we felt was the ideal location — just off of Highway 169 and Valley View Road in Edina. It was perfect. Lastly, we needed to come up with a name. After a bit of brainstorming, we came up with the "Goalcrease" and it just stuck. We were about to take a leap of faith and believe me, I was nervous. Luckily I had no idea what I was in for, otherwise I might have had second thoughts. That first year was going to be non-stop craziness unlike anything I had ever experienced before. I just stayed focused though and kept that vision in my mind of us standing on the ice with a bunch of young goalies for our grand opening. That really drove me and kept me motivated through the good, bad and ugly of what was about to come that year.

We worked very hard for months and months to get everything ready to go. I will never forget the final build-up leading to our grand opening, it was exhausting. It seemed as though we were working for 24 hours straight for several days in a row to get it ready to go. Some of the staff even wound up sleeping there. I remember flooding our ice sheets and painting lines the night before we were set to open and just praying it was all going to work. We were fabricating ice into a building that wasn't designed for that, so we were definitely well into uncharted territory. We had kids scheduled to come in that next morning though and we didn't know what we were going to do if it didn't get set up properly. When we finally got done with it in the middle of the night we were exhausted. Those freshly painted white ice sheets and

Videotaping a Session

blue creases looked so amazing, we couldn't wait to get some kids out there to try them out. When our first clients arrived that morning we were so tired, but it didn't matter. A dream was about to come true.

Since then it has been really rewarding. We have truly been blessed with so many great people who have become clients. It is like a big family for all of us. There have been some bumps in the road along the way though, that is for sure. Things like flooding and re-surfacing the ice, picking up pucks, video-taping, fine-tuning our computer system, ramping up our staff and running our retail shop have all required a pretty big learning curve. It was very intense at first. I didn't think the phones were ever going to stop ringing. But, we figured it all out and were running on all cylinders in no time. Looking back, we are definitely better off today than we were in year one. We are approaching 650 goalies off all ages at the Goalcrease now and that is something I am very proud of. Parents can set up all their scheduling on-line at our web-site and that has freed us up to do what we do best — work with the kids. We keep a great database on each kid in our computer system too, so we can consistently monitor and track their development. It is all pretty state-of-the-art stuff and we are constantly trying to improve every day.

We have a tremendous staff that works here and that is really what sets us apart. The one-on-one attention kids get is just second to none. All of the men and women who work here are former goaltenders who played at a high level and are great teachers. That is really revolutionary in this business. You know, the benchmark for what I would like to be doing here at the Goalcrease is Nic Boleterri's tennis academy down in Florida. It is the best of the best and that is what we aspire to. He started very small and he grew it into an empire which is renowned for being the premier academy of its kind in the world. One thing he realized early on, and this is something I am definitely trying to emulate, is the fact that if you want to really impact kids you need to train them on a consistent basis. So, when kids come down to his facilities for weeks or even months at a time, they are going to walk out of there much, much better. Sure, it is costs money and sure it is a big commitment, but if you want to get the best tennis training you possibly can, then that is where you go. I hope to achieve that same pedigree as time goes by.

Our academy is not a summer camp by any stretch. We are not the typical college campus where parents send their kids to stay in a dorm and play hockey for a week. We are completely different than that. We are on a much more personal level with our clients and we take it very, very seriously. This is all we do and we strive to be the best we can be. Sure, our facility is fun and sure the kids enjoy themselves with us, but we get down to business pretty quickly and make the most of our time together. It is almost symbolic of goaltenders in general. They are more isolated and more individual in their approach. Sure, they are a huge part of the team, but they do their own thing out on the ice and are on an island in that regard sometimes. So, here at the Goalcrease our goalies are surrounded by other goalies and they tend to feel right at home learning from not only our team of experts, but also from one another. It is a special place and that is why so many kids from around the world come spend time with us.

You know, it is an amazing feeling to be able to watch parents come to our facility for the first time and see what an oasis this is for their kids. They know that nothing like this has ever existed before just for goalies and they feel lucky to be a part of it. We have created a very loyal following here and I am so proud of that. I know, however, that as far as we have come in such a short amount of time, we can get a whole lot better in the future. I never want to become complacent, I just always want to get better. We are only scratching the surface so far in this grand vision we have here and I know that there is so much more we can be doing. I get up in the morning and wonder what I can do next to make it better. Whether it is training services or products to our goalies, I want it to be the very best. That is the perfectionist in me. I want to be the best and a biproduct of that will be when our goaltenders achieve success at all levels along the way. I am so proud of our kids when they reach their potential — it may be the varsity, a scholarship or even signing with an NHL club. That is the best reward of all, seeing them reach their goals and knowing that the Goalcrease played a small part in that.

Look, this has to be a win-win or we will be out of business tomorrow. If we are just making money and the kids aren't learning, we are not going to be around very long. When the kids get better they are happy. As a result, we get referrals. That is the formula to success around here. We strive for perfection and for referrals, because that means we are doing our jobs very well. Our business is all about people. We are so blessed to have so many great clients, both kids as well as parents. It is a family-like atmosphere here and that is why we get so much repeat business. I mean, we become a part of a lot of these kids' lives and that is a pretty big responsibility that we take very seriously. Sometimes the kids talk to us about stuff they don't even talk to their parents about because we establish a level of trust with them that is very real. We have had kids come in who have had some rough times at home from things like divorce to even a death in the family. For them, the Goalcrease is like a sanctuary. They love it here and they love the fact that they can come here to learn and have fun. They get attention here and sometimes that is just what they need. When kids don't want to leave, then you know you are doing something right. Seeing things like that it makes it all worth while. We know that we have an impact on kids' lives here and that is something we don't ever

Training at the Goalcrease

take for granted.

For us here at the Goalcrease, our philosophy is much like that of any other sport, it all comes down to fundamentals. We know what the core fundamentals should be — things that we believe in and how we teach them — and that is how we operate. I remember the other day having a mom ask me about when I thought that her 10 year old son would be ready for an advanced training session. I respectfully told her that I thought her son needed to take the basic fundamentals session first. Well, she didn't want to do that, she just wanted to skip that part and go right to the next level. Well, I'm sorry, but it just doesn't work that way. There are no shortcuts in goaltending. You can't bypass the fundamentals. And just because you might have mastered some of the fundamentals at the age of 10, you have to continue to work at them day in and day out because as you get older the games become faster. Your fundamentals have a tendency to break down at that point so you have to continually build them back up at a higher speed. You have to keep building and making them quicker in order to achieve success. Ultimately, you have to pay your dues and work hard in order to get to the next level, plain and simple. You can't buy that, it has to be achieved by long hours and dedication.

We also really stress consistency, which is so important. In fact, we work the same core drills with 18 year olds as we do with 12 year olds. Sure, we do them much slower for the younger kids, but they are essentially the same. It is all about sequencing and speed. We break things down and do some things backwards too, so that each kid learns at his or her own pace. Our goal is to get the students to use their senses and feel is a major focus. A move done correctly should feel a certain way, and visa versa for one that is done incorrectly. Once kids start to recognize that feeling and begin to feel confident with it, then we speed up the action around them so that they start to see pucks coming at them faster and faster. Then we throw in more movement and different scenarios along the way until kids become natural doing it. Once a move becomes instinctive, then that is a big step towards becoming a successful goaltender.

Some of the things that we do very well here at the Goalcrease are watching and listening. Our whole teaching system is based on putting the puck in a certain area and then watching for a break-down. Then, when the break-down occurs, we go back and try to fix it. When kids finally master a certain move, then we simply speed things up and gradually make it harder. We also throw more movements in before they make a save selection. If one or two movements break down before the save selection, then we have to go back and fix the movement. Once we fix the movement then we move on to the save selection, and on and on and on. Making a proper save involves an entire sequence of moves and if a break-down occurs early on, then it can affect everything else down the entire chain. Recognizing those things in the proper sequence is the key. I mean if a kid is out of position and unable to guard against a certain angle, then you know he will be unable to react a certain way if the puck winds up in a certain spot.

We are also very methodical in our approach here and we try to put things into practical terms that kids can understand. We do drills over and over and over until they understand them backwards and forwards. It is also very visual. Videotaping is one of the best tools that we have for that because it lets the kids see their mistakes first hand. The reality is that these kids have a lot of trained eyes on them breaking down their every move in order to help them get better. That is a very powerful tool. My entire staff are all former goaltenders and we understand what these kids go through. That is why we have so much success here, we can relate to the kids because we have truly walked in their shoes. To see how excited they get when it all just clicks for them is awesome.

A lot of young goaltenders get so frustrated because they might be having some problems but nobody can ever help them. Their coaches might be great at coaching, but more than likely they know very little about goal-tending. As a result, goalies get into a rut and can't get out. Well, we can help them because that is all we do. When kids come to our camps they gain so much confidence and that is a big part of goaltending without a doubt. It is so mental and work on that aspect just as much as the physical aspect.

You know, when I got the idea to start the Goalcrease a lot of people told me that this wasn't going to work. They said I was going to lose my money and fail. Well, that was all the motivation that I needed to succeed. And do you know what? We are the leaders in the industry and I can't even begin to tell you how good that feels. Here are some more thoughts and ideas about what we do around here.

CHAPTER SIX:
WORDS OF WISDOM FOR PARENTS OF YOUNG GOALIES

SO, JUNIOR WANTS TO BE A GOALIE...

I remember my mom asking me all the time when I was a little kid, "Are you sure? Do you really want to be a goalie? Are you sure you want to do this? Why do you want to do this? It's not too late to change your mind...". I see this a lot with parents today as well. Usually, they are just shocked that their kids would want to be a goalie. First of all, they don't particularly like the fact that their kid is going to willingly use their body to stop flying pucks. That scares them a bit, and rightly so. Then, they see the pressure that goalies are under and wonder if they are cut out for that. I think parents also know the level of commitment this position takes and before they make the invest-ment, both emotionally and physically, not to mention financially — they want to be sure that junior is on board. Kids change their minds a lot and this position really requires a pretty serious commitment.

My advice on this is that if your son or daughter gravitates towards playing goalie, great, encourage that like you would any other position. Let them play some games and see if they truly like it and see if they are having fun. That is the key, they should be having fun, otherwise it will not last very long. The bottom line for parents though, is that you should always keep your kid skating and learning all the positions — even if they are dead set on becoming a goalie. That will ensure that they understand the game and that they learn how to skate well.

When I was a little kid, when I went down to the rink to play pick-up hockey I loved to skate out as a forward. That was fun. So, in my opinion, parents should really encourage their kids to learn how to skate and stickhandle before they get caught up in learning how to stack their pads and do a butterfly. If a young kid only has goalie skates, that is wrong. They need to learn the basics of every position before they can possibly understand the intricacies of goaltending. If you can, get your kids a pair of both forward skates as well as goalie skates, let them practice on each. If you get them forward skates so that they can skate around with everybody, they will thank you for it in the long run. It's interesting, but when we start teaching young kids the moves and skating skills of goaltending, we can tell right away which of those kids spent time skating out as a forward and which ones didn't. The ones who did skate out pick it up much quicker and have a lot more success early on. They are easier to work with and ultimately, they "get it" way sooner than those who didn't.

So, as a guy who has been around goaltenders now for more than 30 years, I can tell you without a doubt that the best goalies are the ones who are the best skaters. The better they are on their feet, the better they will be in any sport. Period. Even if you are in a small goal crease, the ability to get from point A to point B in the quickest most efficient route is one of the biggest keys to success at this position. Those skills are all honed at a young age by learning how to skate properly. So, kids need to skate a lot and also learn how to stick handle, pass and shoot. They need to understand the basics before they can move on to specialize in something. That is so important. Sure, if they love goaltending early on, encourage it, but not at the expense of learning the complete game.

Eventually, when they get older, they will make that commitment and

The Goalcrease's Video Room

then you will know for sure. The bottom line is that you can't be a successful goalie by just doing it part time. So, at some point kids need to decide for him or herself whether or not they are going to be a goaltender and then work towards mastering the position. Once they make that commitment, then the more support you as parents can give them, the better.

Lastly, I would say this: I think that it is really important for parents to let their kids go down to the park or pond and play with the older kids. That is where they will learn the game way before a coach will teach them anything. Usually, the older kids at the park will play around with the little kids and it is a pretty fun environment for them. Eventually, the park is where they can try out new moves and different things that they might be embarrassed or afraid to do in a game or in practice. With no coaches around, kids can just be kids and that is a really good thing these days. Learning the basics from your friends and peers is "old school," and something that is not as prevalent today as it was years ago. That is kind of sad. Kids today need more unstructured ice time, so that they can just go out and have fun. That is where they learn crossovers, stick handling and shooting. It is also where they build a love for the game.

ON YOUNG KIDS WHO MAY NOT BE SURE IF HOCKEY IS FOR THEM...

First and foremost for young kids getting into hockey is for them to have fun. That should always be the No. 1 thing, no matter what. If kids are not having fun then they shouldn't do it. Period. I have seen kids pushed into playing sports and it can get ugly. Sometimes parents go too far with their kids and that is too bad. I see way too many dads living vicariously through kids who could never possibly live up to their expectations. Communication has to be the key between both parents and kids in order to make sure that they are both on the same page and that they are both having fun. That is the bottom line. Now, if the kids are having fun, then as parents, I would tell you to try to cul-

Getting Fitted at the Goalcrease Retail Shop

tivate their growth. So, what that means is that if your kid comes to you and says that he or she is having fun and wants to get better, then you as a parent have to be educated as to how you are going to help them. You have to be able to search out who can help advance your son or daughter's skill and knowledge. Ideally, you want to find them the best instruction possible, so that they can better themselves as an athlete. That decision requires research and time, so listen for the word of mouth referrals. Look into all the camps and study who is involved and what their curriculum is. Luckily, Minnesota has a lot of options to choose from, so you can afford to be selective.

Sizing Em' Up

As a teacher and coach I can tell you though that this entire process needs to be driven by the kid, otherwise it won't work. I have had a lot of parents come in to talk to me about their kids over the years and sometimes I have to be brutally honest with them and tell them that their kids just don't seem very interested. I will tell them if I think that their kids are not ready for our program because I want what is ultimately best for the kids. It takes a big commitment and a lot of hard work to get to the next level and if kids are not ready to make that commitment, then it is a waste of time and money for everybody. I tell parents all the time not to invest their money on sending their kids to me until they show them that they are ready to make that commitment to get better. Is it hard to believe that a 10 or 11 year old kid will actually say that? No, not at all. I see it all the time. And when that happens, again, that is when a parent has to be able to react upon that and find them the best teacher to help them achieve their dreams.

I want my young goaltenders to be dreamers and to have aspirations. I want them to visualize success and to be able to see that in their heads. That is important and is a big part of building their confidence even before they step onto the ice. Having said that, however, I think it is also really important to get kids focused on what they have to do in order to get to that point. Hockey is a journey, a process, and it has to be done one step at a time.

ON YOUNG KIDS WHO ARE POSITIVE THAT HOCKEY IS FOR THEM...

There are also kids on the opposite end of the spectrum who you can't drag off the ice. I get parents that come in all the time to tell me that their kids just love playing hockey and they don't know if that is always a good thing or a

Staying in Good Position

bad thing. I guess it can be both. I mean I tell them that they probably love their Nintendo games too, but that you wouldn't let them play that 24 hours a day either. I tell them that as parents, they have to make those hard decisions for their kids. Sometimes it is tough. I think kids just need to be kids and it is important for them to play a lot of different sports and to just be able to enjoy their youth. Burn-out is such a huge thing with kids today and I see it all the time. It comes from both parents pushing their kids too much as well as from kids wanting to never do anything but play hockey. No one will ever convince me that it is healthy for anyone to play hockey 365 days a year, no way. It is just as important for kids to be well rounded and to make sure that they do well in school. That has to be priority No. 1 or hockey won't even be an issue.

If a kid is seven, eight, nine or ten years old, I tell the parents to let their kids play all different kinds of sports. Football, basketball, baseball, golf, running and soccer are all wonderful things for kids to do, no question. It will be fun for them to try different things and it will also help them develop a wide range of skills necessary to compete. Being a well-rounded athlete is just as important as being a well-rounded person. They will see early on, however, that being a goalie is a lot of hard work — probably a lot harder than any other sport that they are going to play. And it is not just the physical side of the game I am talking about either, it is the mental side — which is very, very demanding.

Now, for the older kids it is different. You know, you very rarely see a 17 or 18 year old goalie playing three sports these days in school. Goalies have to be focused if they want to succeed at the next level. It is so competitive at that stage of life and that is just the reality of the position. Again, I am not discouraging kids from participating in other sports, that couldn't be farther from the truth. Rather, I am just saying that if a kid wants to be a goalie at the next level, in juniors or in college, then they have to focus on that more than anything else. Of course, not at the expense of their schoolwork or anything like that, but as far as other athletic endeavors go. It is so tough to make it at that next level and the kids who do seem to have this common denominator among them. Kids sometimes need to make tough choices and being a goalie makes some of those decisions even tougher from time to time.

ON $TICKER $HOCK...

I tell parents early on in the process that they need to identify a budget for their kids. I mean playing goalie can be sticker shock for a lot of parents and that is just the reality of expenses associated with the equipment. A lot of schools and associations simply don't have the funds to outfit each kid, especially the goalies. I am realistic with them though and tell them that they don't need to be spending a ton of money on their 10 year old's equipment and development. I know it is tough because the kids all want the "coolest" pads and the ever-popular custom face-mask, but that stuff is not important at that stage of the game. What is important is if the kids are having fun, are genuinely interested, and that they are learning the right things at the earliest stages of the game.

Parents need to be firm with their kids at an early age too. They need to identify a budget that they can live with and then help their child pick out the appropriate equipment as well as the right developmental camps. I think used stuff is great for kids because they are going to outgrow it anyway. It is more important to work with the kid and develop the tools to be successful, versus just getting him or her a bunch of expensive new equipment. Plus, the used stuff is already broken in, which will save you a lot of time and heartache. Now, there is some correlation with regards to kids getting excited about new pads and wanting to play more, but you just have to keep it all in perspective so the both of you don't get burned out. I have seen parents on that end of the spectrum too, where they just can't justify mortgaging the house so that their 10 year old kid can have a custom painted goalie mask. I think parents need to be patient with their kids as well, and gauge their level of interest accordingly. Kids may not be totally into it early on, but one, two or three years down the road they may really start to thrive in that position.

Here, at the Goalcrease, we are always aware of these things and really try to help the parents do what is best for both them as well as their child. We want to help them set up a budget that they can all live with it. Believe me, even though I sell equipment, I don't want to see a 10 year old kid spending three thousand dollars on goalie equipment. That is not right. Stuff like that just leads to false premises about equipment and that is not good for anybody. So, you have to find the right scenario and balance for each kid and your family.

A POSITIVE WAY TO DEAL
WITH YOUTH COACHES...

First of all, it is very important to remember that at the youth levels, almost all the coaches are volunteers. So how critical can we really be? These guys work their tails off and oftentimes get very little respect in return. That is too bad. Most coaches have real jobs and families and we can never take that for granted. The fact that they want to be out there teaching our kids to the best of their abilities should be commended. Sure, they are going to make mistakes and sure they are going to make some poor judgments every now and then. But, 90% of these people are out there for the right reasons and are not appreciated. They deal with so much adversity too. From parents who whine; to kids who don't work hard; to finding assistant coaches to help out; to organizing practices; to the never-ending travel — it can be a full-time job at times. We should all be very grateful to these people and give them the credit that they deserve. And, in the rare event that you get a coach who is out of his or her league and something needs to be done, then please work within your association to respectfully handle the situation.

Now, take in to consideration too, the fact that probably 99% of these volunteers have no goaltending experience whatsoever. That just makes it even tougher for young goalies and all the more reason why they should seek out additional training from a qualified goaltending coach who can work with them. It is a reality that goalies don't get the same attention as the other kids, but that is just the way it is. And, even if a coach does have some goaltending experience, that in no way means he or she is qualified to teach it. I mean instructing the basic fundamentals is a long way from having a passion to teach the position. There is a big difference between teaching and coaching.

The bottom line is this: parents need to learn to deal with their kids' coaches as well as their coach's decisions. They might not always agree with those decisions, and that's OK, but they should learn to respect them. Your kids will thank you for that too. You know, I don't think I have ever met a coach who wanted to play a goalie who he thought was his worst player. Coaches want to win and be fair and they will typically play the kids who give them the best chance at achieving that. Now, at the younger levels, they have a responsibility to let all the kids play. But, if a big game is on the line, coaches are expected to play their top kids in order to give themselves the best chance of winning. So, I think parents need to understand that coaches make decisions, right or wrong, based on their idea of what a good goalie is. Now, that doesn't mean the coach necessarily knows what a technically sound goalie is, because we know that's rarely true. It just means he or she is making a decision based on thier knowledge of the position.

Remember, most coaches have the right intentions, they just might not always make the best decisions along the way. You can't expect a volunteer peewee coach to know it all, he is probably helping out because his kid is on the team and he wants to do the right thing. We need to keep it all in perspective. It is a volunteer system at the youth level and it is not perfect. Yes, there are flaws in the system. If you really want to make a difference, volunteer your own time to help out and then you will understand the pressure these people are under from their own peers. Believe me, it is no picnic.

Parents also need to remember that if they get labeled as "problem parents" early on in their kids' career, that could haunt them forever. I mean if they get upset over their kid not starting a big game or something and then yell and scream at the coach, they are really only punishing their kid. You tell me, how many volunteers do you know have fun getting ragged on by other parents who are unhappy about the amount of ice time their kid is getting? There is a good chance that the coach is not going to forget that and in all likelihood it will just upset him to the point where he will not want to help your kid catch a break down the road. This can especially be bad if you live in a youth hockey association that feeds from the bottom up. I mean if you have a bad rapport with a coach, and yes — coaches do talk and words do travel, you are more than likely going to have problems all the way from mites to high school. I am not saying all coaches hold grudges or anything like that, but some certainly do. Again, you have to remember that youth coaches for the most part are volunteers, so they aren't about to take a lot of flak from a bunch of loud mouthed parents. I mean let's face it, you could triple their salaries tomorrow and they would still make zero.

So, choose your battles wisely and remember the political ramifications of your actions. Sure, things get said in the heat of the moment and we all wish we could take some of those things back after they are out there. In my opinion, the best thing a parent can do is just sit back and think about what they are going to say to not only their kid, but also his or her coach before they say it. If you are not sure what to say, sleep on it and then ask another goalie parent what they might do. Remember, this is a marathon not a sprint. If your kid struggles early on or catches a bad break from a coach, just hang in there and keep working hard on both their fundamentals as well as their attitude. The important thing to realize is whether or not your son or daughter is progressing, learning and having fun. That isn't always measured in wins and losses, don't forget that.

The same is also true for referees. Refs take so much guff from parents and coaches these days and I think it is just terrible. They are human too and it seems like people are not treating these people with the respect that they deserve. I mean do you really think that by yelling at the ref that he is somehow going to give your kid or your team a better call? No way. In fact, it is probably going to have the exact opposite effect. And what kind of example are you setting for your child, yelling at someone in public? So, the moral of the story is that if you want to get your point across to either a coach or a referee, do it in the right context and please try to do it with respect. You will get a lot further in pleading your case and your kid will thank you for it in the long run. I guarantee you that if you go up and thank a person for volunteering their own time to help your son or daughter, that you will have a lot more

Practice, Practice, Practice...

success with them in lobbying your objective. If you tell them how much you appreciate what they are doing and then articulate how a different approach motivating your son or daughter might be beneficial — you could be shocked at the results. They will respond much better to that versus the other alternatives.

We see parents getting so caught up in a game that didn't go well for them. They need to understand that three or four years down the road nobody will even remember that game. So, keep it all in perspective and try to focus on the long term good of your child. One game will not make or break your kid. The big picture is about your goalie having fun and wanting to put in the time to become better. Work with the their coaches and try to be their ally, you and your kid will enjoy the process much, much better in the long run, trust me.

Parents need to have knowledge, that's first and foremost. You know, it seems like all parents think that their kids' situation is so unique — and that may very well be the case, but over the years I have heard it all. Oftentimes I will hear things from parents such as: "My kid doesn't have a goalie coach and they are feeling very lonely…" or "No one is paying attention to him and he's struggling and frustrated..." or "My son is feeling isolated because the other 18 kids on the team are spending all the time with the coaches and he is being left out." They tell me that they are paying the same amount of money to have their kid in youth hockey, yet they feel shortchanged with regards to how much their kid is actually being coached.

While I agree with them and sympathize with them, I also sometimes feel like saying that they probably don't realize how lucky they really are. Then they look at me like I must be crazy. Hey I understand, you want someone to be working with your kid to help them improve as a goaltender. But more often than not the coaching that's there is not great. Techniques and coaching philosophies are passed down from generation to generation and they're not necessarily what is right for today's kids. For example, when I was a kid we never wore seat belts while traveling in the car. That was then, and obviously things are much different today. Incredibly, back then that's all we knew. We just didn't realize how important seat belts were for our safety

Working on the Basics

and how they could save lives, so we went with the flow. Now, we are educated, and wear seat belts because they save lives. Well, some of that analogy is true in goaltending as well. A lot of the old-school goalies teach the game the way they were taught. As a result, a lot of old techniques and philosophies are continually passed down to new generations of kids. I mean sure, some of the fundamentals are timeless. But, many things in regards to teaching have improved greatly over the past 10 years, and those methods have not yet been accepted. So, in a lot of ways we are still back in the Dark Ages. So, sometimes no teaching is actually better than outdated philosophies.

There are a lot of inefficiencies built into the system and that's just the way it is. For parents to become really upset with that and to get bent out of shape isn't going to do anyone good. Getting upset and staying focused on negative energy is just bad for everybody. Sure, it might be tough to see your kid get benched for a crucial game, but you just have to encourage him or her to hang in there and keep working. Goalies are always going to share their position, much like pitchers in baseball. There is almost always a tandem, or rotation, of kids who are going to play, so it is important for them to realize that they have to be positive team players. If they are not playing that night, then they need to support the other goalie who is, and be ready to go if their number gets called. Attitude is everything in goaltending and that starts at home with mom and dad.

ADVICE FOR YOUTH COACHES...

The first thing youth coaches need to remember about coaching young kids is that they are just that — young kids. Young kids, for the most part, are not very coordinated athletes. So, they have to be very patient and encourage them to focus on improvement, all in a context which the kids think is fun. That can be tough sometimes. Coaches need to understand that it might take several years before kids evolve into good hockey players. But, they also need to know that what they are doing at that particular point in their kids' development is crucial. They should also remember that kids at the youth levels are still pretty fragile. So, they need to be cognizant of what each kids' situation is and try to deal with them accordingly. I mean a kid might not be developed yet physically or they might not have the best situation at home with their family, and if you push them too hard you might just drive them away from the game altogether. They need to be sensitive of those things. Just try to think about how you would want your son or daughter to be treated by their coach, and then you will do and say the right things.

I think coaches also have to careful of "over-coaching." It is really easy to do. What I see a lot of times is where coaches tend to over-coach in those big games where there is a little more pressure on the line. As the season becomes more and more significant, coaches become more and more critical of their players, especially their goaltenders. This can be dangerous. They may tend to focus on things late in the season which are more conservative. This may be natural for coaches at all levels of the game, but it's dangerous to start tinkering with a goalie's psyche at this point of the season. If things are working and he or she is playing well and appears fundamentally sound, then take my advice: "don't fix what aint broke." Here's what I mean, in a big playoff game you might casually mention one or two extra things to your goaltender that you hadn't mentioned all year. Now, they might start thinking and that can be dangerous. It is a mental battle with goaltenders and you need to recognize the right and wrong times to address changes with them. If a goalie starts thinking about changes to his or her performance more than usual, their reactions will slow down and now you've got a problem on your hands. So, for coaches, I believe coaching less in big games is better in the long run. Say the right things and let them relax, that's when they will play their best.

One bit of advice I would have for youth coaches is when you have a young goaltender who is seeking out additional training on his own, don't go against the grain. Just help them develop. Encourage growth and accept the learning curve, that's how they become better. Furthermore, and I say this with all due respect, if goaltending is not your strong suit as a coach, you need to understand that just throwing him or her in goal all practice to stop pucks doesn't necessarily mean improvement. Sure, facing shots and getting in shape can be good, but goaltenders need special coaching to help them move in the right direction. Otherwise they can pick up many bad habits that will be tough to break later. So, if a kid wants to seek out additional training, support them and embrace it. As a former goalie, I would say that you are lucky, A) if your goaltender has a passion for the game and wants to learn more, and B) is seeking guidance from a professional whose main goal is to build their foundation. This will ultimately allow you to focus on what you do best with the other players on your team.

I really believe that youth coaches should take the time to try to edu-

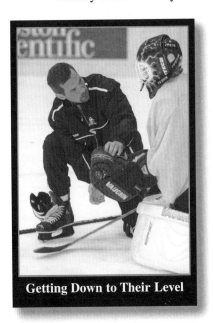

Getting Down to Their Level

cate themselves on the fundamentals of goaltending. Read a book, check out a good website or even get an instructional video. All of those things will help and they are readily available. You will definitely help your young goaltender's confidence if you take an interest in their development and can work with them on specific things other than just being a target in drills that are primarily aimed at helping your forwards and defensemen. And hey, if your goalie lives in an area where he or she can come to a camp or an academy, then embrace it and consider yourself lucky that their parents are finding expert training on a subject that you may not be an expert in.

One of the things that bothers me the most is when I hear stories from parents on how coaches get frustrated with the learning curve and wind up just telling their young goaltenders to "forget about what you are learning at camp...". I mean that is just wrong. For instance, a kid might be working on a technique and struggling. Well, he might let in many goals in the process and instead of the coach recognizing that the goalie is trying to improve, he just says "forget about it, go back to what you used to do...". That's selfish, short-term success and it will hurt not only the psyche and confidence of your goalie, but it will also hurt your goalie's chance of being better at the end of the season. I can't tell you how many goalie parents tell me how they're frustrated, and rightfully so.

They know that if they address this with the coach that they could potentially be labeled as "problem parents" so they often grin and bear it. Not only are they frustrated about their son or daughter's lack of skill development, but are also frustrated that their investment in training could go to waste as well. So, we do our best to talk to coaches and let them know our teaching philosophies and encourage them to work on those same things in practice. Smart coaches will quickly figure out that by working together, it's like they have their own personal goalie coach, for free. We can be a resource for them and can work towards a common goal. Our goals are mutually beneficial — we want that kid to get better so that he or she can help their team become more successful.

Nothing irritates me more as a goalie coach than to hear a youth coach admit that they know very little about goaltending, yet they will turn around and instruct thier goalie to do something which is completely outdated. For goodness sakes, please! If you don't know much about goaltending, that's OK. Don't feel bad, the vast majority of coaches don't. But ask for help whenever you can and try to educate yourself. Don't stand in the way of a goalie's development because you may lack knowledge. When we hear coaches speaking from both sides of their mouth, we have to take a deep breath and address the problem by talking to them. First we listen and then ask questions. Before long we get a feel as to what the coach is trying to accomplish and then we try to work within their framework to accomodate them. We want to make sure that the goalie is progressing and learning the skills necessary to compete.

Another piece of advice that I can recommend for coaches of goaltenders is to encourage footwork. That's where it all starts, with their feet. If you want to help your goalie get better, improve their skating skills. Many coaches just bombard their goalies with shots and don't realize the value of skating drills, thinking it will tire them out. I disagree. Goalies need to be in great shape, first of all, and beyond that they need to have good footwork. You can't stack your pads, do a kick-save or execute a butterfly without having that. Have them skate, skate, skate, it's so important. They may not want to, but they need to. Then, you want to follow that up with movement drills specifically designed for goalies.

Besides footwork, another area which a coach with very little knowledge can help is with angles. This is half the battle, just being in the correct position to make a save. If a goalie continually gets beat in a certain spot, they'll eventually need to make an adjustment. A good coach can help their goalie make that adjustment by being observant. Coaches should skate around and study where his or her goalie is set up, keeping an eye on where they are getting beat and when they are making correct saves. Compliment them when they do it right and work with them on making adjustments to their angles when they do it wrong.

Another problem we see a lot is goalies leaving their feet too early and often. This is very common with young goalies who haven't developed thier skating skills. Going down often represents of a lack of confidence and that will improve as thier footwork strengthens. But, a coach needs to work with their young goaltenders in order to help them determine which situations are best to leave their feet and visa versa. Most kids are'nt great skaters and simply have not taken enough shots on their feet in order to get the correct perspective of timing. Initially, their first tendency is to leave their feet. So, as a coach, what you can do is run more drills (specifically sharp angle shots) where you keep them on their feet and just work on it over and over until it sinks in. It takes time and patience, but your goaltender will catch on sooner or later. He or she will eventually process which save selections are most appropriate for each instance. As they get older and more patient, that thought process happens in the blink of an eye. If a skater dekes one way and shoots the other, going down to your knees is a part of goaltending — it's just determining when to go down and in which situations.

Believe it or not, we still see a handful of coaches who played back in the 60's. That era of goalies didn't wear facemasks and never wanted to leave their feet. If they played on their knees, they would have been hit in the face with many pucks. I guess some of it is a generational thing too. Today, the kids are so well protected that they don't have that issue. So, it is all about finding a balance between the two. I also don't think it is good to be labeled as a stand-up goalie or as a goalie who goes down a lot either, you should be able to do both and do both well.

Chillin' at the Crease...

Another thing that I highly recommend for coaches to do is to encourage their goalies go out and watch other good goalies in action. That's so important. They need to be able to visualize things and see firsthand how their peers play the game — both good and bad. They will inherently pick up the good stuff and try to emulate it. When I was a kid I used to watch goalies on TV and in person, studying their every move. Whether it was Donny Beaupre and Gilles Meloche with the North Stars or whoever was in net for the UM-Duluth Bulldogs or Gophers, I just wanted to see the best of the best whenever I could. I could hardly wait to arrive early for warm-ups, I would stand behind the net to watch the goalie during warm-ups. To see how he played his angles and to watch his footwork, it really gave me something to strive for in my own game. Having other goalies to watch, whether they are heroes or mentors, is a good thing for young goaltenders.

So, if you are a youth coach, get your kids over to see an NHL game, a college game or a local high school game. Tell them to watch and learn and not just screw around with their friends. Have them watch the goalie's every move and study what he is doing when the puck is in the other end. Tell them to visualize themselves in the net on a breakaway or on a two-on-one and then predict what they might do in the same situation. They will learn a ton and it will expose them to all different types of environments. Better yet, encourage them to go out and watch a college practice. I guarantee you they won't complain about the length or difficulty of your work practices after that.

Occasionally we find ourselves in the odd position of being in direct competition with our kids' coaches. And when I say competition it is really more like a contradiction in the sense that we want to teach our kids a philosophy of goaltending which sometimes is exactly the opposite of what his coach has been teaching him. This can be tough. A kid knows that if he wants to play that he has to listen to his coach. But, if that coach is teaching him a method which is out-dated, then we feel like we need to teach the kid the newest and most efficient way to do it, otherwise he will develop incorrectly. It can be a struggle of wills between us and the coach, but ultimately we will talk to that coach and explain our rationale for what we are doing. Usually at that point they agree that we are the experts in this field and that we are only trying to get the young goalie to develop the right habits for his long term growth.

At the Goalcrease, we are all about teaching kids our common sense philosophy towards goaltending, and also about trying to teach the coaches the right way as well. Then, when they go home they are all on the same page working together towards the same goals. That is what it is all about. Lastly, coaches should never think that what they are doing is not worthwhile, because it is. We are all grateful for your contributions to our kids, you are making a positive difference in their lives. Thank you.

ON DEALING WITH THE POLITICS OF HOCKEY...

Good or bad, politics have been and will always be a part of youth sports. That is just the way it is. The way you deal with it, however, is crucial. We hear so much negativity all the time from parents who complain that their kid isn't getting enough ice time, or that they're not being treated fairly. Well, that may be true, but you need to make the best of your situation. Otherwise, I think you should get the heck out and do something else. Life's too short and being miserable isn't an option. If it gets to be too much and it's too stressful or too political, then just opt out. Brutal? You bet. Hockey is a tough sport and many kids get weeded out early on because of that. If you can't enjoy or deal with the politics or the travel and the expense of it all, then encourage your kids to skate for the fun of it. Encourage them to play other sports and to have fun and to do well in school, that is the most important thing in all of this. If they love hockey and want to do it, great. But if it affects other aspects of their life such as your relationship or their grades or their home environment, then leave the game on your own terms. This is an intense position and it is not for the weak of heart I'm afraid.

If your kids like to see results without the politics of most team sports, then encourage them to play golf, or wrestle, or swim, or run track. Those sports are pretty cut and dry. If you run a 10.9 in the 100 Meter Dash and the next guys runs an 11.2, then you win. If you shoot a 69 on the golf course and the next guy shoots a 72, then you win. It's pretty straight forward. In wrestling, the guy who beats all the other kids in his weight class in practice that week gets to represent the team on the varsity. The coaches kid has no outcome in that decision whatsoever, it's all on the kids to see who is the best and which one works the hardest to succeed. There's not much politics there, and a lot of people gravitate towards those activities because of that. Hockey, however, is a very subjective sport that relies upon a group of coaches, many of whom are volunteers trying to do the right thing, to make some difficult decisions with the hopes of fielding a competitive team. Add in the fact that kids start playing this game at a very early age as well as parents who are emotionally involved, and it can be a political nightmare at times.

Again, this is not a perfect system by any means. Every kid, no matter how talented, will go through rough stretches and have to deal with politics along the way. Usually, the cream rises to the top and if your kid works hard and stays out of trouble, they will be fine. This game was meant to be enjoyed by both the kids as well as the adults, we can never forget that. Hockey can be the most positive thing in your son or daughter's life and it can

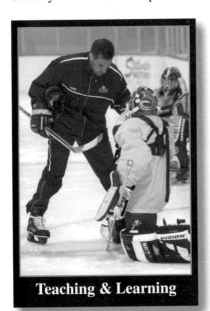

Teaching & Learning

also be the most negative if the situation gets out of control. Hockey teaches kids about the values of sports; how to get along with other kids; how to handle adversity; the virtues of hard work; and how to be a leader. These are wonderful qualities that can be used for the rest of their lives. Focus on the opportunities the game of hockey can provide, not the politics.

So, parents need to detach themselves from their ideology of what's right and wrong, and encourage their kids to remain positive in the eye of the storm. If you are negative at home about their coach or their situation, then I guarantee that you will be sabotaging your kids' athletic future. Eventually they will buy into that ideology and they will quit. I have seen it so many times. Remember, it's just a game. All parents want what's best for their kids, so it's up to you to keep it all in perspective.

When it is all said and done, there's only so much parents can do for their kids. If they want to achieve success it will come from hard work and no one should hold their hand with that. I can't tell you how many times I have asked a group of goalies the question: "How many of you want to be great?". Do you know how many kids raised their hands? Twenty out of twenty, every single time. Then, when I asked that same group of kids how many of them went home the previous night and worked on the drills that I had assigned for them to do, do you know how many raised their hands? Maybe two or three. I asked how many of them did the dry land training exercises such as doing wind sprints that would help them develop quicker footwork; if I have a group of 100 kids, maybe six will raise their hands. So, it's easy for kids to say they want to be great, but the fact still remains that most kids just don't put in the time and effort to be great. It is as simple as that.

As a teacher and coach this is very frustrating. When parents tell me that their kid is coming out on the short end of some politics, I am compelled to ask them how their kid prepared for tryouts. Did they run? Did they lift weights? Did they do any plyometrics? Did they study the materials we assigned for them? Did they go the extra mile to get better? Their silence is usually enough to answer the question. They usually follow that up with "Yeah, but he or she is so talented and the coach just cut the wrong kid..." I don't know, did he?

I want the responsibility right back on the kids and I want them to take ownership of the results. Sure, parents are involved, but if kids want something then it's up to them to make it happen. As a parent, you can help your goaltender control certain things: his work ethic; his preparation; his dedication; his mental attitude; his physical being; and his nutrition, then you are going to be all right. In fact, you are going to be great, and on top of that you are going to enjoy it. Look, not every kid is going to make the A team and that is just a cold hard fact. But, good things happen to kids who work hard and that's no coincidence.

If you really want to make a difference as a parent, then enjoy the process and leave the game to your kid. Sure, give your kid the tools to help themselves, but then relax and encourage them to have fun. In the end you will both have a much better overall experience. Nobody says doing that will be easy, especially if you are not happy about your kids' progress, but it is the right thing to do. Recognizing that is important, because from there you can then articulate how you want to help your child from behind the scenes. Yelling and screaming will get you nowhere, that much I can promise you. I remember vividly when I was a kid and my parents started getting too involved in my games and I just hated it. It was very uncomfortable. When they were more or less out of the picture, that is when I really had the most fun. I remember being a kid and wanting to make the team on my own merits. That was so important to me. That way, if I made it, it was my own doing and visa versa — if I didn't make it, then it was on me and only me.

Sure, parents have made a lifelong investment in their child's future — emotionally, physically and financially, and they want to see a return on that. I get that. But they have to go about achieving that in a healthy way. There has always been politics in hockey, the two go hand in hand. But the game can still be fun.

ON "HOCKEY MOMS" & "HOCKEY DADS"...

It's amazing, but parents will feel the same stressful emotions while watching their mite or squirt play in goal as when he or she plays in high school or college. That feeling of watching them stand in goal as an opposing player skates down on a break-away is just as nerve racking for mites as it is NHLers. Parents will know that they are officially goalie moms or dads when they are watching a game and it is tied late in the third period. The stress you feel and the stress you know that your son or daughter is feeling at that exact moment is an emotion only you can identify with. Being a goalie parent is something you can't exactly describe, it's just a special bond you share with other goalie parents. The pressure is what separates you from the other hockey moms and dads.

You will also see that as your child climbs the ladder and advances on to higher levels, that the pressure also rises accordingly. Parents need to grow as their kids grow, so that they too can deal with the pressure effectively. It's important that parents learn how to manage stress and pressure so that they don't bring it home with them. That's so important. If you bring that baggage from the rink into the home, it can be detrimental to not only your kids' attitude, but also your own personal relationship. I mean taking a bad loss home with you is so unhealthy. And believe me, kids can sense if you are dealing with the pressures effectively. In reality, most kids forget about a bad game shortly after the car ride home. They are on to the next thing, whether that is school or video games or playing football or whatever. The bottom line is that parents need to do some soul searching in order to strike that balance. Ultimately, if they can do this the process will be more enjoyable over the ensuing years. This isn't an option, it's a must.

Laura Working Hard

Let me put something into perspective. Just because your son or daughter has put in the time and hard work, a la training throughout the off-season to get better, then often the parent's sense of entitlement increases. While I can understand that rationale, it doesn't always gaurantee a spot on the team. I know that is tough to deal with sometimes, but that is reality. I mean every parent loves his or her child, and they obviously want what is best for them.

So, when all the expensive training doesn't pay expected dividends, things can become sticky. Oftentimes, instead of just supporting them, they push them in a "tough love" kind of way, too far and it becomes counter-productive. They just need to back off a bit, support them, and point them towards success. Over-bearing parents mean well, but can wind up hurting their kids in the long run. They wind up trying to fix a coaches decision, something that can't be fixed. They care about their child's well being and they have a lot invested into the situation both emotionally as well as financially — so there is a lot on the line for them in their eyes. The fact of the matter is no matter how well you prepared, it won't guarantee a starting roster spot on the A team, the high school team or a college scholarship. There are just no guarantees in this position.

In my opinion there are two types of parents. There are the parents who have supplied their son or daughter with the most opportunities that they can (i.e. taken them to the most amount of tournaments; bought them the best equipment; and have done the most amount of driving time to away games, etc.), and feel totally invested. For them I think having fun is only a part of the bigger picture. Now, the other kind is the mom or dad who will simply drop their son or daughter off at the rink and leave them there for the afternoon to play with their friends. They go and do their own thing and then come back to get them by the end of the afternoon to pick them up. Those types of parents will simply ask their kids if they had fun and will not read much more into it. There is a big difference between these two types of parents. I am not saying one is right and the other is wrong, no way. I am just pointing out that there is a big difference philosophically between the two — that is all.

I do think, however, some parents get too attached to their kids' lives when it comes to sports, it can be a bit too much. If their kids don't turn out like they hope they will, in terms of athletics, then they need to be supportive of them nonetheless and just let them have fun. Overbearing parents can be detrimental to kids, not just in sports, but in everything, and that is sad to see. When they are too attached to their own dreams and aspirations, then that can be totally unhealthy. I understand that every parent loves his or her kids and that they want nothing but the best for them, but sometimes they just take the wrong approach in achieving that. I have seen it all in my experiences as a player and now as an instructor, and it is unfortunate. Having said that though, I think those parents are definitely in the vast minority and that for the most part parents are doing a great job with their kids. Hey, I am lucky, we get to teach some great kids here and we have met a ton of great parents as well. They have surprised me. You know, one thing I have learned over the years is that good kids usually come from good parents. That is the truth.

Because goaltending is such a difficult position to master and because there is so much pain and frustration that goes along with winning and losing, things can get frustrating for both the kids as well as their parents. For some parents though, I think that when things sometimes don't go their way, their first natural instinct is to protect their son or daughter. From there, they usually lash out and blame the coaches and then blame the developmental program — basically trying to find a reason as to why their kid is struggling. As a parent myself, I can certainly understand those feelings. But, parents have to realize that the only person they are hurting by doing that is, ironically, the one they want to help the most — their son or daughter. So, as parents we need to detach ourselves from those emotions and it will be more fun.

I see so many goalie moms and dads just pacing like crazy people torturing themselves up in the stands during games and it is difficult to watch. They are so nervous and about ready to explode. So many of them just can't enjoy the games anymore and that is sad to see. Believe me, I have been there and can tell you first hand that it is not fun as a goaltender to see your parents or loved ones biting their knuckles all night. Quite frankly it can be really distracting. I don't necessarily know the exact answer as to how each parent can detach themself from that outcome, but they just have to work at it and figure it out for themselves. You know, if you can't, as an adult, detach yourself from that end result and if you feel like you are not going to be in control of that situation if things don't wind up working out the way you were hoping them to, then the solution is simple — don't go to the game. It's that easy. Just drop your kid off and go have a cup of coffee. Really, if you can't handle the pressure of being a goalie mom or dad, then just stay away and it will make things a lot easier for everybody — especially your son or daughter. Believe me, you will do more harm than good if you show up in that state of mind. That can be detrimental to your kids' psyche.

A lot of goalie moms and dads spend the game in the bathroom. I hear it all the time that parents "watched the game from the bathroom…". Well, of course you can't actually see the game from there, but that is where they wind up in order to just get away. That way they can escape from the pressures of the action without having to watch it, and they can even throw up if they want to while they're in there. It sounds crazy, but that happens more often than you think. It's funny, but I recently asked my mom if she too was like that up in the stands while I was playing. She looked at me and started laughing. "Jeez Robbie, I was a nervous wreck… you are just lucky I didn't die of a heart attack up there watching you!" Luckily for me she hid it so well, she was just a rock.

Another thing that is brutal, and I see it all the time, is after a tough loss parents will wait around until their kid is all showered up and ready to go and then they start to coach them in the car ride home. This is not the time nor your place to do this. That does more harm than good. Parents don't want to criticize them and make them feel worse, but because they are so attached and invested into the situation, they can't stop themselves. It is just so unhealthy too, I cringe when I see that happening because the long term ramifications on the kid can be serious. Then, we, at the Goalcrease, wind up spending the next day, week, month or year trying to build that kid's confidence back up so that he or she can get their edge back. Again, being positive at home is half the battle, believe me.

It also amazes me when parents will say negative things about the team goalie. Are you kidding me? Don't you realize that people talk and it will eventually get back to the parents of the goalie, or worse yet, the goalie himself? And let me tell you something, the last thing you want is a goalie worrying about whethor or not everyone is questioning his ability to keep the puck out of the net. Parents have to learn to keep their thoughts to themselves, or they can really hurt a goalie's confidence. They are fragile young kids and if their confidence is shot, they are doomed. It is tough. I mean a goalie can let in three goals and still win a game. Each time a goal is scored though, he might take a verbal pounding from the fans. And I am not even talking about the opposing fans, I am talking about his own team's fans that want to win. Then, if he winds up winning that game 4-3, all is forgotten and he is the hero. It is so hot and cold. You are the hero and the goat several times in any one game. Parents just have to learn how to keep it all in perspective and never get too high or too low. Each player has to deal with the pressures that come along with the position on his or her own terms. That is all part of the equation, and why playing goalie is so much tougher than any other position on the ice.

I know there are a lot of parents reading this and shaking their heads right now, knowing that they have been there and have been a part of these things first-hand. They have been in the stands and heard terrible things being said about their son or daughter. They have been isolated, both in the stands during the game, and afterwards, in the arena lobby with the other parents. Nobody wants to look at the goalie's mom or dad. It is sort of surreal. The other parents' body language sometimes says it all. Welcome to the goalie parent's fraternity!

It is hard enough for a young goaltender to have to deal with the thought of letting his teammates down after a tough loss. It is even harder for that same goaltender to have to deal with the thought of also letting down his parents and his friends' parents. So, recognize what he or she is going through and think about what you either want to say, or not want to say. Sometimes it is best to write down what you want to say and then talk about it the next day, when the emotions are not so intense. Whatever you do, don't say something you will regret on the car ride home.

Focus...

ON TRAVEL...

Traveling is definitely one aspect of the game that makes hockey unique. If you have a son or daughter who is already playing the sport then you know what I am talking about. Hockey is a lifestyle and if you are not on board with all the weekend tournaments, then you better find some parents who you can trust who will look after your kid. The bottom line is that kids will travel quite a bit at the youth levels and most of it is not school sponsored — meaning there are usually no buses or vans, just parents loading up the kids and taking off. You know what though, it can be really fun. Embrace it. Find some other parents who you like and try to hang out with them. Dinners on the road in strange small towns can be great. No, you will probably not like each mom or dad on the team, but try to make the best of it and life will be a lot better for everybody. If you are lucky, you just might strike up a fantastic conversation with your teenager in the back seat — something otherwise impossible at the dinner table.

When I was a kid up in Duluth we traveled all over the place. It wasn't uncommon for us to spend a weekend in Fargo one week and another in Thunder Bay, Ontario, the next. Part of the reason why we traveled so much was because we were pretty rural and needed to physically drive in order to play different teams which presented really good competition. Kids in the Twin Cities for instance, might not ever have to travel. So, it is a case by case thing that you will have to deal with as it presents itself. Just know going in that you will definitely be doing some traveling with your kids if they play hockey. It has been that way forever and it will be that way forever. Pack up the van and make the most of it, otherwise you and your kids are not going to have a very enjoyable winter.

ON PRACTICE...

Practice is so important, I can't stress that enough. That is where it all starts for kids and if they are serious about hockey then they need to be serious

Coach Ostby Holding Court

about practicing. That is where their work habits are formed and where they learn to play with their teammates. It is also where they bond with their teammates as well as earn their respect. In fact, I really think that kids need more unstructured practice time these days. They need more time just to go out there and have fun with no coaches around. Again, that is where kids learn to be creative with the puck and how to try new things without the fear of either being embarrassed by the teammates or chewed out by their coach. But, with the explosive growth of girls hockey today, there is less and less ice time to go around for everybody. As a result, a lot of youth associations can only have ice time either super early in the morning or super late at night. To make up for the lack of practice time, I think they are scheduling more games instead. Then, less quality practice time for the kids to practice the fundamentals and iron out their mistakes results in poor play across the board. I mean are 30-40 games too much for an 11 year old? Absolutely. Should parents have to drop everything so that their kid can play in a four game tournament every other weekend? No way. If you want to have a say in this stuff, then be vocal within your youth association, otherwise deal with it in a way that won't hurt your kid.

My vote would be for less games and more quality practices — especially on outdoor ice. When I was a kid that is what we did. We skated outside and we loved it. And, it was free. Unfortunately, however, the days of kids wanting to practice out in the cold are over. Kids now are really spoiled and don't want to play outdoors. Sure, they might go out on the weekend to play a little pick-up at the park, but they don't want to practice out there when it is really cold. Hey, nobody likes to freeze. But that is what made us so good — we embraced it and made the most of it. You can't be good in games unless you are good in practice, period. Look, the reason The Goalcrease exists is for this very reason. We provide that quality practice time, only exclusively for goalies. So, something has to give there. That was one of the things that Herb Brooks really wanted to see, more outdoor rinks being built inexpensively. He challenged the powers-that-be to think about building 10 quality, lighted outdoor rinks, some even with artificial ice, for $2 million, versus one nice arena for the same amount. He was on to something. Sadly, when he died so too did his voice for getting that done.

ON BREAKING DOWN FILM...

We do a lot of videotaping at the Goalcrease. This is an extremely valuable tool that has really changed the game. But, and this is the key, you have to know how to A) shoot the film properly from the right angles; and B) be able to break down and understand the film in the proper manner. Hey, if mom wants to take out the camcorder and shoot her kid in net for an entire game, that is great. Junior can then watch it over and over and try to figure out what he did right and wrong. The fact of the matter is though that most kids don't know what to look for when they are studying tape and it can be counterproductive if it is not done correctly. If parents don't know the proper techniques to analyze that footage either, then leave that to people like us who can look at it and use it as a tool to help their kids get better. I mean when we video-tape kids we breakdown moves frame by frame so that they can see what is happening. That is incredibly powerful. In fact, we can even teach goalies how to recognize certain situations and then instruct them on how to actually stop goals before they are even shot.

I would also recommend that mom stand behind the opposite goal-tender at the rink and record from that angle so that you can see the entire ice sheet. You need to be able to see how plays break down in order to fully comprehend positioning and angles. Don't fixate on your kid the entire time, shoot the whole game by following the puck around. Let your kid learn about all the different aspects of the game, not just what went on in the crease. A well rounded goaltender is like the quarterback out there and he or she needs to understand what everybody else's role on the team is too. That way he or she can position his or her defensemen on a face-off and know who needs to be where when there is a defensive breakdown. Again, let your kid go over the tape with a coach to pick up things that went right or wrong. I just don't think it is healthy for mom or dad to do that unless they are qualified to do so.

Another thing about film that can potentially be bad is when you review game film and only go over the negative stuff. That can be detrimental to a goalie's confidence. You need to make sure you compliment the good saves, praise the adjustments and recognize good positioning. Don't just focus on the goals that were scored or it will be counter-productive to what you are trying to accomplish. I had a goalie coach up in Buffalo when I was playing with the Sabres who did that to me and every time I walked out of his office after reviewing film I felt terrible about myself. The guy just crushed my confidence by doing that and he didn't even realize it. There is no value in that. There is value, however, in praising the good things and encouraging your son or daughter to work on their weaknesses in a positive way. Sure, point out their mistakes, but do it in a constructive and positive way.

ON TOUGH LESSONS...

I remember one time when I was about 11 or 12 years old and we had a practice outside. To my horror, I looked in my bag and realized that I had forgotten my goalie blocker. I ran over to my dad and asked him if he could please drive home to get it for me. Well, he was all about teaching lessons and simply threw me an old chopper instead. He knew that I was about to learn a valuable lesson; stay organized and don't forget your equipment. I had to play the entire practice with this ratty old mitten instead of my blocker. I just had to toughen up and deal with it. But, I did learn my lesson, albeit the hard way, and do you know what? I never forgot my blocker again — a simple but valuable lesson.

It amazes me sometimes to see just how many kids forget their skates and what-not at games nowadays. I am not sure that letting them miss a game or two isn't the worst thing in the world for them. Kids need to learn lessons, sometimes the hard way, and that is the truth. Too many parents let their kids get away with too much I think and sometimes that just enables the kids to be lazy. If they know that mommy will just run home and get what they need whenever they need it, or even run over to the sporting goods store and buy them a replacement piece of equipment on the spot if they are on the road at a tournament, that doesn't bode real well in the hard lessons department. Kids need to learn how to be responsible at a young age and also to be accountable. If they miss a game sometime on account of the fact that they got lazy, then you can be pretty sure that they will double check things in the future.

ON THE "BLAME GAME"...

Goaltending is perhaps the most stressful position in sports. There is immense responsibility and pressure placed on goalies to perform. When adversity arises, too many goalies relieve themselves of that pressure by placing the blame on others. Everyone knows goalies need to have a positive outlook, but playing the blame game is entirely negative. The blame game is not the solution to the problem.

All of us involved in hockey play the blame game. The first is the goaltender himself. How many times have you witnessed a goalie throwing his or her arms up in the air after a goal is scored through traffic, tips, or screens? When I see this happen, my first reaction is that the goalie wants everyone in the stands to know that he or she is not at fault: or "Don't blame me, I couldn't have done anything different to prevent that goal."

This type of reaction prevents a goalie's growth. Every difficult or impossible play must be viewed as an opportunity to become a better goaltender. Just because it was difficult to locate the puck does not mean it could not have been stopped. Throwing one's hands up insinuates that nothing else could be done to prevent the goal, and that is not reflective of a champion or a leader. Pointing the finger at your teammates destroys team spirit and isolates you at a time when unity is key.

Parents are also expert players of the blame game. Too often they cast blame on their son or daughter's teammates by telling them that the defense played terrible; the defense did not clear the rebounds; and games will not be won when only one goal is scored. Such attempts to make your goalie feel better after losing do not promote growth. Trying to soothe your goalie's pain after each loss by blaming his or her teammates does not solve the current problems that caused the outcome. In cases such as this, just being mom or dad is good enough. As a parent, you don't have to take the pain away. Instead, being positive and offering

Using Robb's Patented "Staubar" Learning Device

hope, by saying "Tomorrow is a new day" or "The sun will still come up tomorrow" is far more effective then blaming anyone. It's very easy to blame someone else as a parent. For most, saying maybe my son or daughter needs to get better is much harder.

Finally, coaches excel at the blame game too. How many times after losses have you as a coach critiqued the preparation of your team? I suspect not nearly as often declaring "We need better goaltending." In my 30 years as either a goaltender or goaltender coach, usually it is assumed that the goalie is at fault. And perhaps you are correct with all your coaching expertise and your goaltender may in fact not be very good. If so, however, then one must ask, what have you as a coach done to make your goalie better? If your answer is little, then don't be so quick to point your finger at the goalie because there are three pointing right back at you.

Granted, blaming your goalie makes a coach feel better. And doing this has the added benefit of deflecting criticism away from you as a coach because you can hide behind the fact that you never played goalie and you do not have the expertise to help them. The truth is that blaming the goalie does not solve the coach's and team's problem. Why does a 12-year-old, who has played goalie for two years deserve to be blamed for lack of experience and inadequate training? We must realize that young goalies simply are just not that good yet. Lest we forget, as a coach it is your responsibility, and honor, to see that your goalie gets the specialized training necessary to make him or her successful.

Here is my challenge to goalies, parents and coaches alike. Let's leave the blaming to all those who need to make themselves feel better at somebody else's expense. Let's take a better approach and assume there are no problems, just solutions. In today's world there is plenty of blaming but not nearly enough working respectfully together to make things better. Let's do our part to keep hockey special and unique. Let's stop the blame game and help our goalies and all of our athletes become better not only in hockey, but as citizens better prepared for all of life's adversities.

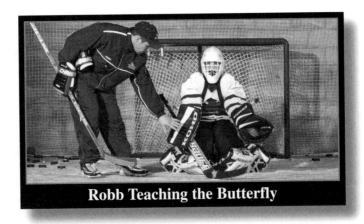
Robb Teaching the Butterfly

ADVICE FOR PARENTS OF
HIGH SCHOOL AGED KIDS...

I think the most important thing here is for parents to just back off. If you are going to get involved, be positive. You know, I have seen more kids come in over the last couple of years with similar situations in that their parents fill their heads with so much negativity. It is interesting to see how much things change for younger kids when they turn 16 and are able to drive themselves into our facility without their parents with them. When they come in on their own we never hear negative things from them. Wow, it is like night and day when you remove them from that environment. Then, without all of that negativity clouding their heads, they can just focus on improving and on having fun. That's what it is all about. When we see our kids laughing and smiling, we know that that we are going in the right direction. That is half the battle in making a difference.

I hear so much negative stuff from parents these days that it is almost sad. Parents come in and tell me that things are so bad for their kids. Everything is bad, bad, bad. They complain about coaches not being fair; about how their kids are not being used effectively; and about how they feel their kid is getting the short end of the stick. It is truly amazing how much kids' attitudes change once their parents stop micro-managing them. We see so many kids start having a lot of success and making big personal gains when we don't see mom or dad around — what a coincidence! I am not telling parents to not be involved once their kids get older, no way. I am just saying please be careful what you say to your kids and don't be afraid to let them go to practice alone sometimes. The entire dynamic will be different and sometimes that can be healthy.

ADVICE FOR PARENTS ON THE
TRANSITION OF THEIR KIDS FROM
HIGH SCHOOL TO THE NEXT LEVEL...

When I deal with parents of kids this age I am very clear to refer to them as adults. Because if your kid is good enough to play at the next level, then they should be treated as such. My advice to you is to let them learn to deal with the situations that come up regarding their own careers. That is all part of it. At this level there are no mommies or daddies calling the coach to whine about their kid not getting enough ice time. Believe it or not, coaches tell me all the time that some parents actually do do that, but it is usually laughed off. This is big-time when kids get to this level and while there is some luck involved, for the most part it is safe to say that yes, the best usually are at the top. That is the reality of playing at the next level where all of the kids are elite players. Frankly, I think most kids would be horrified at this point if their parent called up the coach to complain or whine about ice time. That, would almost certainly be detrimental to their kids' career and would almost guarantee diminished or no additional ice time. Coaches at this level are paid employees and they have a job to do, which is to win. Sure, they want to develop kids and they want them to graduate and all of that, but the only way they are going to keep their jobs is by winning. So, they don't have to put up with the crap that the volunteer youth coaches do. Parents just have to tough it out and let their kids handle those situations when they get to this level. I mean would you call his or her boss if they are having trouble at their job? Of course not, and the same is true in hockey at this stage of the game.

ADVICE FOR PARENTS OF KIDS WHO WANT TO PLAY JUNIOR A...

If your son is 18 or 19 years old and he is thinking of playing juniors, here is what I would recommend for him to do. I would tell him to really, really study and learn how to make adjustments in every aspect of his game. They need to use that time to perfect their game so that they will be able to have a shot at making a good D-I or D-III college team. With that comes a lot of pain and a lot of growth, but it is completely necessary.

Now, take a young kid who has just made a Junior A team, and he is looking ahead to his future — I don't think enough of those kids spend that year or two getting better. They just become survivors of the position, so to speak, without making enough adjustments to really better their games. They are just so afraid that if they have a bad game or two, that they are going to get benched. So, kids are reluctant to try new things to really get better at this level almost out of fear. In my opinion, however, kids need to do just that, they need to take risks and try to expand their games in order to get better.

It is so critical at this level to have several "styles" to adapt to different opponents in different situations. I believe the biggest mistake young goalies at this level make is that they come in already thinking that they have a "style." Let's face it, there is a big reason why they are playing juniors at this point and why they are not playing pro hockey. It's because they aren't good enough. Period. So, they need to work hard, study and learn as much as they can in order to get better in every facet of their game. They have to improve their game not just on the ice, but off of it as well.

Glove Technique

Honestly, I don't see enough of that. I think too many kids get way too comfortable in what they are doing and don't expand their minds in order to get better. Sometimes you have to take one step backwards in order to take two steps forward and that is so true in goaltending. It is uncomfortable and even scary to try new things out there, but without taking chances you will never truly get better. Every single kid has to go backwards before he can go fore-word and the sooner kids understand that, the sooner they will be able to take that next step. Most kids don't even have a clue as to how good they can real-ly be if they just did these things. So, when I see kids come in and they tell me that they have a "style," I just have to shake my head because I know I am going to have my work cut out for me. I am quick to tell them that at the age of 18 they are still at least 10 years away from becoming a good goaltender. That is just reality.

ADVICE FOR PARENTS OF KIDS WHO WANT TO PLAY JUNIOR B...

This is a developmental stage and an important transition between high school and college. To that parent I would tell them not to worry about any of the recruiting stuff until the season is over. Encourage your kid to stay focused, work hard and have fun in high school. Weighing your future options at the age of 18 and with no scholarship opportunity can be trying, but it can also be very rewarding. From there, encourage your son to do some research on all of the teams through the internet and have him find out which ones might be the best fit for him. Find out which ones have had goalies graduate up to Junior A and then into the college ranks. Those are all really important things to know. Find out which teams have assistant coaches and which ones have specific goalie coaches. Do everything you can to help your kid to make the best choice for himself so that he can find success. If your kid just wants to play at that level for fun and has no desire to go on, then that is OK too.

Junior B can either be a great stepping stone to Junior A, or it can be a place to hang out and have fun playing hockey with your friends too. Just make sure they know what they are getting into and how much of a commit-ment they are going to have to put forth in order to achieve whatever level of success they want. You can call coaches at this level and contact them direct-ly to find out as much as you can. You need to be proactive, however, and recruit the coaches as much as they recruit you or your kid. Things that will help will be putting together a good video and then following up with letters, e-mails and calls. It is a process that can take time to find the right fit, but one that can be very rewarding in the long run.

There are so many goaltenders out there and for the most part, the ones who are the most persistent are the ones who are going to be picked up. The guys who get picked up are the ones who will go the extra mile. They are the ones who are not afraid to tell those coaches "Hey, take me as your third goalie and give me a chance to prove myself...". They just have to get their foot in the door any way that they can. From there they have to work their butts off and hope things play out. Hey, it is all on them to work hard and put themselves in a position where they can catch a break. Don't worry about if they are going to be the No. 1, No. 2 or No. 3 guy on the depth chart.

Don't worry about any of that, just tell them to get their foot in the door and go to work. That is the best advice I can give high school kids who want to continue on but don't have a scholarship or reasonable walk-on opportunity waiting for them. There are no guarantees at this point either, just opportunities and, yes, a little bit of luck. Remember, don't make any demands on the coaches, just tell your kid to stay relaxed, work hard and have fun.

You know, I see so many kids who really want to continuing playing after high school and for many of them Juniors is a good route. A lot of them though figure that if they don't make it at the Junior A level then they are not going to even give Junior Bs a shot. I think that says a lot right there. Sure, Junior B is not as sexy as Junior A, but it is ice time and it is a path to take to prove yourself and graduate up to the next level. It can be a good stepping stone if a kid wants it badly enough, that is for sure. They need to show them that they are a "late bloomer." I have seen kids start out in Junior B and prove themselves well enough to get to Junior A and then wind up playing in college. So, it can be done. It is all about attitude at that point and the kids who want it the most usually wind up excelling at this level. The fact of the matter is anytime you are playing competitive hockey after high school, you are doing pretty good. Hey, most of the other kids are either playing in late night bar leagues or have their equipment stuffed in their basement somewhere collecting dust.

ADVICE FOR PARENTS OF KIDS WHO WANT TO PLAY FOR A DIVISION III SMALL COLLEGE PROGRAM...

As kids climb the ladder they need to understand just how few kids there actually are playing competitive hockey. It's not that many. The higher you go, the fewer the opportunities there are because there are fewer and fewer teams for them to play on. Kids going on to play at the D-III level are in a good situation though I think. This is a different ballgame for the most part. The vast

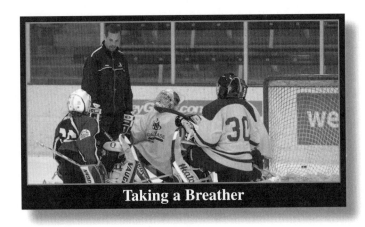

Taking a Breather

The Lovely Laura Can Make Anybody Laugh...

majority of people here understand that they are not going to be playing beyond this and therefore they have a different attitude about the entire experience from the onset. They understand that their careers get shorter every day and playing D-III hockey is all about fun. I think kids at this level clearly know that the NHL is not in the cards, so they are getting their educations while still playing competitive hockey. By the time these kids are 21, 22 or 23 years old, they will be ready to enter the real world and be able to get good jobs. Hockey at that point will either be a great memory, or a Sunday night tradition with their old pals. This is a really good option for a lot of kids and one I think more kids should think about. Hey, enjoy the wins; enjoy the losses; the bus trips; the locker-room conversations; the practices; the fans coming out to see you; everything; because once you start working 40, 50 or 60 hours a week at a real job, you will look back fondly at those times and really miss them. I guarantee it.

ADVICE FOR PARENTS OF KIDS WHO WANT TO PLAY FOR A DIVISION I MAJOR COLLEGE PROGRAM...

Let's say your son or daughter has a few options on what they want to do and where they want to go to play hockey. First of all, congratulations, your son or daughter is among the very best of the best. However, as a parent, the best advice you can give your kid is to help them help themselves so that they make the best educated decision for their future. With regards to programs, research them and find out as much as you can about them. The first thing is to find out about the history of each program and about their development in that particular position. Research which goalies have played there with success or failure and then ask questions as to why they were good or why they were bad. Don't just look at who has the best team and won the most, but which program would be the best fit for your son or daughter based on their playing style as well as coaching style. If your son or daughter doesn't get motivated by a coach who yells and screams and runs boot camp practices, then discourage them from going to a place like that. If a certain program only plays one kid at all costs and never develops the other goalies in a rotation, then that may be something to factor in too. You need to look at it objectively and then determine a game plan as to which option will provide your kid with the most opportunity for growth, that is the key. Again, it is not about who has the best program (i.e. the winningest), it is about who has the right program for your son or daughter. If you are lucky enough to have options, then you have to do your homework in order to find the best fit for growth. If they get into the perfect situation, then the sky is the limit for playing in the professional ranks.

Now, about kids who are hell bent on making a D-I roster. For these kids I would just say this; you had better work your tail off in order to get better because you are no longer the best kid on your team. This is the big time. Kids who want to play at this level need to have that desire to work so much harder than the other guys. They will have to step up their games big time and set higher and higher goals. Then, they need to go out and achieve those goals. They had better be prepared to make a lot of sacrifices along the way too, because it is no picnic getting ready to try-out at this level.

Having said those things, I would also say this: Kids who show the talent and desire early on to have a chance at playing D-I need to make a lot of adjustments while they are young. I can't tell kids this enough; make those tough adjustments while you are young because every year that you wait to do it will become harder and harder. Trust me, it is much tougher to "teach an old dog new tricks" at 19 than it is at 17 and it is even tougher at 21 than it is at 19. Making changes to improve your game is tough, but absolutely necessary. Coaches want kids who are versatile and can adapt to different opponents. The more open minded your son or daughter is about learning new things, then the better off they will be down the road. Being a student of the game is so important, I just can't stress that enough.

CHA-CHING!

DID YOU KNOW THAT NO LESS THAN THREE GOALCREASE PROTÉGÉS WERE SELECTED IN THE 2005 NHL ENTRY DRAFT?

1) JEFF FRAZEE (2nd Round, New Jersey Devils)

2) ALEX STALOCK (4th Round, San Jose Sharks)

3) JOE FALLON (6th Round, Chicago Blackhawks)

THE "STAUBAR"

The Staubar is a patented teaching device that I invented in 1999 to help kids better understand proper positioning and technique. We make it mandatory for our kids here at the academy and it has become an integral part of our training philosophy. You see, it is difficult to try and break experienced goalies of bad habits and it's just as frustrating to stop young goalies from developing those same poor habits — habits that wreck havoc with fundamentals of stance, balance, movement, and positioning of arms, hands and sticks. It is the first goalie training device directly conceived using principles of human anatomy, kinetic energy, and muscle memory. I am really proud of it because I know it has helped a lot of kids.

No matter what style a goalie uses, the more of themselves and their equipment that stays squarely in front of the shot, the higher the odds that the goalie will stop the puck. Therefore, the Staubar puts more of the goalie in front of the shot, which ultimately creates "high percentage" goalies. It's designed to "force" goalies into the habit of moving everything they've got squarely in front of the shot. In fact, it's anatomically impossible for a goalie to move any other way. When wearing the Staubar in practice, a goalie can't repeat improper technique, get lazy, or rely on their athleticism to flick out a glove or blocker. The Staubar trains good sound habits and technique, making it reflexive to move the entire body squarely toward the puck. By regularly incorporating it into practice sessions, proper technique becomes a habit that proceeds without control of the goalie's conscious brain. The Staubar cements a reflex that just begins to "feel right."

Training with the Staubar creates a chain reaction of energy efficient kinetic movements and puts a goalie in the best possible position to stop the puck. This how the Staubar Trainer works:

INITIATION: When wearing the Staubar, the goalie must initiate every move from the inside edges of their skates.

DRIVE: Pushing off the inside edges forces the knees to bend and drives the legs toward the puck.

SQUARE: The leg drive forces the goalie's body and shoulders to move square to the puck and the Staubar forces the goalie's hands into positions squarely in front of the body.

POSITION: When body and equipment are square to the puck — with the hands squarely in front of the body — the goalie is in the best "high percentage" position to cover more net and block more pucks.

HANDS: Because the Staubar forces the hands in front of the body, the goalie is cutting down shooting angles. Plus, the hands are in position to poke-check, react to tipped shots and control rebounds.

BALANCE: With a square stance and hands in front, the goalie is balanced and ready to make the initial save, as well as, prepared to move in any direction to cover a rebound.

MEMORY: Muscles have memory and muscle memory gets stronger through repetition. That's why training with the Staubar regularly, turns proper technique into reflexive habit.

ON MY OWN UNIQUE STYLE...

I definitely had a style which was all my own. I believe on some levels that goalies are entertainers. I mean when I played, the more I could excite people the better. That motivated me. When I came skating out to the blue line to challenge a skater, that got the crowd totally fired up — and as a result that got me fired up to play better. I took risks and did a lot of daring things. That was just me. Most goalies didn't take that approach but I think that is what made me so unique. I caused a lot of coaches to have near heart attacks I am sure, but for me it was about having fun and winning. I was on my own man out there and did whatever it took to get my team the edge. If that meant skating all over the place and putting it all on the line, then so be it. I never understood why so many goalies just sit back there and wait for the action to come to them. I loved to skate and I viewed myself as the sixth skater, not just a backstop. If I could get to the puck and get it to a forward breaking out, that was awesome. I loved getting assists, that was the ultimate. When I was playing in the minors and I scored a goal on an empty netter, that was definitely one of the highlights of my career.

Playing aggressive in goal was a huge advantage for my team too. To have an agile goalie who could skate and pass the puck across the ice, defenses can't account for that. In some ways I would like to think that I did change the game that way. Not too much, but in a small way I think I revolutionized the position a little bit to make it more offensive. Sure, I got burned more than once skating out to the blue line, and it is a lonely place to be when the skater gets past you and has an open net to shoot at, but that is all a part of taking risks. If they are calculated risks, then they usually work out more often than not. But not all the time and that is part of what was entertaining about my style — you never knew just what was going to happen.

I also loved the fact that other teams never knew what they were going to get when I was out there. It kept them a little off balance and that gave us a small psychological edge I think. I loved to push the envelope every now and then and just have fun out there. That kept me loose and motivated me to succeed. From the moment I stepped onto the ice I couldn't wait to get out of my crease. I liked to be different and I liked to entertain. It all went into who I was as a player. The vast, vast majority of goalies all play exactly the same way, and that just wasn't for me. The key was finding a coach who had enough confidence in me to give me a leash that long. Once I had that, it was all down hill from there.

You know, being a goalie is a lot like being a kicker in football. You are usually either the hero or the goat and there is not much middle ground. Some guys can't hack that kind of pressure, but I liked it and was able to channel it. That is why I was good at it.

ON MY TEACHING AND COACHING PHILOSOPHY...

I take coaching very seriously. I make sure that my kids know why two plus two equals four. Anybody can memorize the answer, but I want them to understand it and get it. I work really hard at teaching them the fundamentals and then I explain to them why they are doing those things. For instance, I tell them why their hands have to be out in front of them when they are in proper position: 1) You have much better balance; 2) You cut down open net behind you; and 3) You can make better recoveries. I don't just tell my kids to do something and have them do it. I educate them. I explain why they need to do it and then I show them, both in person with them out on the ice and then again on slow motion videotape. Then they get it and they understand it. I base a lot of my fundamental teachings not only on personal experience, but also on great coaching that I received along the way, as well as on science. Goaltending is angles; it is geometry and physics; it is making adjustments; it is understanding how to put your body into the right position at the right time in order to be successful. I constantly tell my kids that they are never done learning in this position. Even when I was in my late 20s and playing professional hockey, I was constantly making adjustments and trying to get better. So, when I get through to kids, they know why two plus two equals four. It is not just a memorized habitual response to them, it becomes a learned equation that makes sense.

I really enjoy teaching at all levels, whether it is little kids just starting out or at the college level, where I currently serve as the goalie coach for at the University of Minnesota. Over the past several years I have been fortunate to work with a couple of top notch goaltenders in Adam Hauser, Justin Johnson, Travis Webber and Kellin Briggs. I used to design special programs and drills for those guys all the time to correct problems that they might not even realize existed. You don't want to mess with a goaltender's confidence if you don't have to, so you need to constantly think of creative teaching methods which help solve your student's

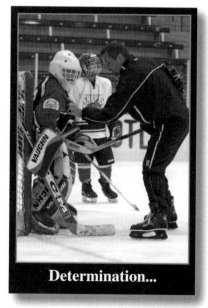

Determination...

Getting Down and Dirty

problems in the best way possible. Sometimes I don't want guys like that watching game film and thinking too much. That is my job, to break down the film, and then I will work with them on fixing their problems or bad habits in a way that I feel is best for them.

Everything about this position is mental, whether you are playing it or coaching it, and you can never forget that. As a coach, if you do something wrong, you could totally mess up your goalie's self confidence and then you are in big trouble. As a goaltender, even if you have lost your confidence during a game, you can never show that emotion. Not only will the other team smell blood and come in for the kill, but your teammates will lose confidence in you too. So, coaching these guys is a process and you have to be smart about how you decide to handle various things. You also have to be very careful on how you criticize them too, because that can be traumatic and have serious consequences down the road. The bottom line is this, in game situations you don't want your guy thinking about techniques and game film and things like that, you just want him to react. My job is to help him tune everything else out and just focus on that. It is also my job to be there for those guys through the thick and the thin, as their friend, coach and occasionally, their psychologist. Sometimes that means dealing with problems from the roots, like dealing with their parents.

I remember talking to Adam Hauser's parents after a tough loss one time. We were having a discussion about Adam and about some of his ups and downs that he was going through. I was trying to get them to back off of him a little bit and maybe get them to look at his situation a little differently. I really wanted Adam to be able to figure out his own problems on his own this time. That is a very important lesson to learn in goaltending. Well, his mom then proceeded to tell me that when my own children were older and in that position some day, then I would know what she was talking about. She told me it was hard to understand, but that as his parents, they knew what was best for him. She told me that they felt strongly about how they were advising him.

I think it is easy for parents to want to get in there and try to solve their kids' problems. It is easy for them to go to the coach and to try to make everything better. It's hard for parents to watch their kids make mistakes. I know that they don't want them to feel any pain or to do poorly and struggle. Here's the deal though, parents can't protect their kids all the time, especially in this position. The psyche of a goalie is very fragile and sometimes they need to take their lumps in order to figure out their own problems. Once they do that, then the sky is the limit. Then it becomes fun and burn-out is not going to even be on the radar.

I know that when Adam finally did get things corrected in his own mind, on his own terms, it probably sunk in a whole lot more because it was all his doing. That is a very empowering feeling and something that does wonders for your confidence. Playing goalie is so much about self confidence and about the ability to fix your own problems when they come up. Goalies have to multitask so much out there and then on top of that they have to deal with the overwhelming pressure of it all. Sure, everybody needs coaching and support, but sometimes when things are down you have to just gut it out and come up with the answers on your own in order to grow as a person and as a player. Sometimes I think learning the hard way is the best way.

So, I sat back respectfully and listened to the Hausers. It was not my place to tell them how I felt about their son. I just wanted to give them my advice as a coach and fellow goaltender. I had been through the meat grinder on more than one occasion and it was my job to help our goalies to get better. I have been a goalie now for more than three decades, so if I can pass along some of my wisdom to the next crop of players, then that is a legacy I would be very proud of.

You know, when I went to the University of Minnesota I never dreamed of ever winning the Hobey Baker award or winning any award for that matter. No way. I only thought about all of the great goaltenders who had played in goal before me and how I was ever going to live up to that. My goals coming to college were never about setting records or winning awards, they were only about winning and about being the best goalie I could possibly be. Well, later on when I began coaching at the U, it was really a thrill to teach Adam Hauser and to see him break a lot of those records. I was really honored to have been a part of his college career. It meant a great deal to me, to be able come back as a teacher and pass on my knowledge to someone who shared many of the same goals that I had. Records are meant to be broken and it is great to have them broken by a guy you are mentoring. His success and growth as not only an athlete, but as a person, was so fun to watch. Then, when they won the National Championship in 2002, that was just an unbelievable experience. For me, to come so close back in 1989, that was a tough pill to swallow. So, it felt really special to be a small part of it that time around.

We won another won that next year with Travis Webber and Justin Johnson in goal and that was awesome too. To have them both under my wing was an unbelievable experience as well. My approach was the same with all of those guys: let's be the most consistent; let's be the hardest working; let's control what we can; and let's just get better. The three of those guys were all great goalies and the common denominator with all of them was the fact that they were persistent. So, to win it all in back-to-back seasons, something that hadn't been done in college hockey in more than 30 years, was pretty incredible.

Lastly, I also think that from a coaching perspective that it is easier to be more critical of a goalie when he or she is winning. Then, you are teaching and motivating them when they are in a different mindset. When you complain to your kid while they are in a slump, that is a tough place to try and get through to someone. I think a great example of that was articulated by Paul Ostby in Ross Bernstein's book about legendary coach Herb Brooks:

"Herbie's methods of motivation were really unique," said Ostby. "You know, we have a tendency in our society as coaches and as people that when things are going well, we pat people on the back and say 'great job, way to go.' Then, conversely, when things are going poorly, we get real negative. Herbie was just the polar opposite of that. For him it was all about reverse psychology. So, when things were going well, that is when he put the heat on and asked for more — because that is when an athlete or a person is most receptive to that kind of psychology. Then, when things were going poorly, he would back off. Now, sure, sometimes they needed a kick in the butt, but for the most part he would ease up on them when they were down."

ON THE SUCCESS OF THE GOALCREASE...

I always tell parents whenever I am asked that the biggest reason kids should come to the Goalcrease is because we teach. We teach. Period. We break kids down and we make them better. We study them, work with them to pick apart their bad habits and tendencies, and then we fix them so that they can become better goaltenders. To get better we have to constantly get more creative in our thinking so that we can adapt and improve. We never want to become complacent so we are always studying new techniques and discussing how they will apply to certain kids. We try to customize each kids' sessions so that they improve on the things that are the most important to them. It takes time, but we are committed to our kids and we are committed to giving them quality one-on-one time in order to get the job done right. We teach kids to play goal and that is totally different than tweaking them, which is what most week-long Summer camps do. Well, I can tell you with great confidence, you shouldn't tweak an eight year old, you should teach him. That is all we do and we do that every single day here.

We have had some kids at the Goalcrease go on to have success at different levels and that is so gratifying to see. It is absolutely wonderful to watch those guys develop into even greater players and to see them doing well at the next level. Honest to goodness, I have as much enjoyment out of watching one of our kids having success and doing well as I did getting a shut-out in an NHL game. It is different, but just as exciting and rewarding. Take Matt Lundeen, who was the Metro Goalie of the Year and the Frank Brimsek Award Winner last year, he got a full-ride scholarship to Maine. That was so great to see. What a great kid. There are so many others too, like Justin Kowalkowski, who played at Blake High School and got a scholarship to play at Colgate; or Joe Fallon, who got a scholarship to Vermont; just to name a few.

We have really been making a difference here and it is starting to show. Thirty five high school goalies trained at the Goalcrase in 2004-05 and of those, 19 finished in the top 30 statistically in the state of Minnesota. That was just awesome to see. I mean there are over 400 goalies playing high school hockey in the state and we had that many elite level kids wanting to work with us. That is what is all about for us. We can't wait to pin those statistics and articles up on our bulletin board. We cut out stuff and post it because we want our kids to see success so that they in turn will visualize success. When they have success, we have success. We measure success differently with each kid that sees us, but we are committed to each one of our kids in the same way, regardless of their talent level. We just want them to get better and to have success in whatever they are doing. They are not all going to get D-I scholarships and then go on to play in the NHL, no way. So, we understand that and set realistic goals for each of our kids so that they can get better at whatever level they are at — whether that is making the squirt B team or the high school varsity. We just want them to reach their potential, that's it.

You know, when I or anyone of our staff gets an e-mail or a nice note from a parent or coach saying that they have seen a big improvement in their son or daughter, or player, that just validates all of the hard work for me. When they tell me that they have seen an improvement in their confidence or in their self-esteem, that gives me goose bumps. I just can't hear that stuff enough because that is why we are doing this. No matter how bad my day might be, a letter or note like that is like a drug for me, I love it.

I got a call recently from a 21 year old kid the other day who flew in from Las Vegas and spent a few weeks with us to get ready for his tryouts out there. Well, he called me right after his tryout to tell me thanks and that he had never ever been more prepared or felt so good about his game in his entire life. Wow! I was just floored that a kid would call me long distance to tell me that, but I tell you what — it felt great. To know that I played a part in this kids' success was just wonderful. To hear the confidence in his voice and how happy he was, was so awesome. I mean as a teacher what else could you ask for?

It has not all been a bed of roses for us though, no way. For me, I tend to take things very personally and will defend something to the end if I believe in it. People need to know that my heart is always in the right place and that I really care about my students. If anyone ever insinuates that we are only doing this for the money, that really hurts. It just infuriates me. Those people don't know me and they really don't know what we do here. Because if they did, there is no way they could ever say that. You get that though, and that is just part of the business. There are a lot of other camps out there and they are all battling for the same pool of goalies, so it can be extremely competitive at times. We don't focus on negative stuff at all here, we just do our thing and know that if we are doing our jobs well then kids will want to come back. Success breeds success and that has always been our motto.

One of the guiltiest aspects of what I do is the fact that I have to charge a fee for what I love to do. I think back to all of my youth coaches in Duluth and how much time they spent teaching us kids. They were all volunteers and they did it for the love of the game, that was it. So, I try to give back when I can and also volunteer my time. The bottom line is that there is a cost associated with our services, but we feel like we have a superior product which justifies that. We hire the best people and have the best facilities to train our kids. It is not for everybody and we are clear about that. We don't want to be for everybody, we just want to focus on a small number of kids and give them a ton of one-on-one attention so that they can play to their best possible potential — whatever that might be. I make no apologies for that, we are a business, but we are also very passionate about what we do. We love what we do and we love our kids. Their success in not only hockey but in life is what really motivates us to be our very best.

My life's work is invested in the Goalcrease and I live and breath it everyday. I have invested into the advancement of goalie development and take great pride in knowing that the Goalcrease is also providing a fantastic career for seven full-time employees. I am committed to them and their families and I am committed to my business. This is my life. I am a workaholic, I admit that. We have a state-of-the-art training facility that I am so proud of and it is just fantastic to be able to have the resources to finally teach kids the way they need to be taught.

And if you think the costs are that much different, look at the numbers. Look, we charge $90 for a 40 minute session, and that is our most expensive package. I would like to see another instructor do better than that. Do the math. To rent an hour of ice at any arena in town is going to cost a minimum of $100 - $150 per hour, on top of what the instructor's fees are, which are probably about the same. So, we think we are an absolute bargain for what kids get here and we make no apologies for striving to be the very best of the best. I am a very competitive person and I want to be the best at whatever I do. Helping kids is what I do now and I want to be the very best at that. That is my goal and I take that very seriously.

I love the fact that we have to prove ourselves everyday here. We are no different from our students. We better be sharp everyday; we better be prepared everyday; we better have enthusiasm everyday; we better be willing to think of and try new things everyday; and we better never get to comfortable with ourselves, or we are going to get cross-checked right onto our butts in a heartbeat. We have to prove ourselves everyday or we will get complacent and fail. We can never forget that or we are dead in the water. We just need to keep getting better everyday, period.

Look, we get it. We understand what it is like to be a goalie because we were all goalies who played at a very high level. I have been there, personally. I have lived it and seen it all. We all have. I have been there when it was lonely; I know you don't get help; I know it is the least coached position; I know it is requires the most amount of pressure to deal with; I know all of those things and that is why I do what I do. Goalies know that if they come to us they will get the attention they need. I want to make a difference and I know that our kids do get better and they do go on to have success. That is so gratifying to know both personally as well as professionally. We have the commitment and passion to help these kids, and helping them to get better and reach their potential is our mission, plain and simple.

You know, we actually like it when our kids go to other goalie camps.

We want them to see what else is out there so that they have a base to compare us to. We are confident enough in our people and our facilities to know what it takes to be the best. We know that they will be back. We are convinced of the fact that one week long goalie camps don't work. I have been there and did that for 10 years. You need to train with a lot of consistency to get better and that is what we offer. That is what it is all about. Week-long camps are fun; they are social; they provide an environment where kids can meet other kids and hang out away from home; they are Summer camps. Sure, kids learn and they provide a service. Again, that is not us. No way. We are dead serious about goaltending and about kids reaching their potential.

Hey, we too are fun and we have a great facility where kids love to come and hang out. But make no mistake, we are very, very different from the other guys. As our kids say, "This is goalie heaven…" And do you know what? The parents love it here too. They come there and it is like they are amongst family. They can talk to all the other parents and it is like one giant support group. They know exactly what they are talking about and can totally relate, whereas other hockey parents don't have a clue about goalie issues. It is comforting for them to come there, to learn about goaltending and to gain self confidence about how to deal with their kids the right way. That is what it is all about.

As for the future of the Goalcrease? One of the neat things we are doing now is getting entire youth hockey associations signed up to work with us. What is so great about this is the fact that now all of the kids in the entire program are on the same page goaltending-wise. When we start with mites and squirts and teach them the basics, they follow those same guidelines into peewees, bantams and high school. Coaches then have the luxury of knowing that each goalie that comes through the system will be taught consistently the same way by goalie experts. This lets coaches focus on what they know best — coaching, and not having to worry about what they are doing right or wrong with their goaltenders. It is a real win-win scenario and we are getting requests from a ton of associations throughout Minnesota to sign up for the program.

Eventually, we would like to become a full-service shop in that we will have an agent working with us to help guide our goalies into the professional ranks doing contract work, financial management and that sort of thing. Hey, it is all about trust in this business. So, it only makes sense for us to offer these services so that we can guide our clients all the way up the ladder — as high as they can climb. We want to be there with them for every step of the way. What a thrill it will be to coach a kid from mites all the way to the NHL. That will truly be something incredible to be a part of. I can't wait.

ON DROPPING THE GLOVES…

I don't condone fighting in any way for kids, let me be very clear on that. In the pros, however, I think it does have a place and it does serve a purpose. I think that when two grown men both mutually agree to settle their differences out on the ice, then that is fine. Where fighting gets a bad name though, are when you have the rare incidents like what we saw happen last year with Vancouver's Todd Bertuzzi. He broke the honor code and as a result he got a big-time suspension and fine. He hit a guy from behind and didn't fight fairly, that is why such a big deal was made out of that — and rightly so. Fighting allows the game to police itself and at the NHL level, that is good for the game. If you had a five-foot-eight guy running players twice his size out there knowing that nothing was ever going to happen to him, then that would be awful for the game of hockey. So, this way problems are dealt with out on the ice and then resolved by the players themselves.

As for me, I was lucky. I never had to fight while I played pro hockey. I was roughed up a few times, but I never dropped the gloves and squared off with anybody. The fans love it when there is a goalie fight, but it is pretty dumb when you think about it. I mean trying to fight with all of that stuff on is just ridiculous. I think it is more for show sometimes. Even now at the Junior A level, there is so much fighting. I just think it is wrong to see kids beating each other up at that level. I mean most of those kids are trying to get college scholarships and just want to play. Sure, being tough is great and it will help, but come on. They wear half-shields in Juniors and then put on full masks in college, so what is the point. There are hardly ever any fights in college hockey because of that, so it is kind of silly in my opinion. I think part of it is due to the fact that a lot of these small towns in Iowa, Nebraska and the Dakotas need to sell tickets in order to make money. So, by having the kids fight they know that the fans will come out to watch it. It's a bad situation if you ask me, and it seems to be getting worse.

ON MY THOUGHTS ABOUT THE 2005 NHL LOCK-OUT & THE ENSUING RULE CHANGES WHICH FOLLOWED...

Let's face it, NHL goalies today are some of the best athletes in the world. They are also getting better coaching than ever, and as a result scoring has been down league-wide for several years now. So, to me it just seems absurd to punish the goalies for doing their jobs better than they have ever done before. Sure, have some goaltenders pushed the envelope by getting the biggest pads possible in order to cover the most amount of space? Absolutely. (Hey, goalies are the smartest guys on the team, so they will always look for "loopholes" to the rules like when Hall of famer Tony Esposito of the Chicago Blackhawks sewed netting in his crotch to seal off his five-hole. Atta-boy Tony!)

But the equipment manufacturers have gotten smarter too. For instance, nobody can really get their knees flat on the ice, so they built leg pads which are shaped better to compensate for that. One new rule which is really going to be tough is where goalies are now going to be limited as to where they can go behind the net. That is going to really handcuff a lot of guys like me who liked to come out of the net and play the puck. I mean let's be honest, shrinking their padding is not the only answer to the much bigger

THE NEW NHL RULE CHANGES FOR GOALTENDERS:

Equipment dimensions will be reduced by approximately 11 percent: including shrinking the trapper's perimeter to 45 inches; trimming two inches off the blocker; reducing the width of the leg pads by an inch; and tailoring arm and chest protectors and pants to each goalie. The pants and jersey also will be reduced in size as well. (The NHL will also enforce cheating by sending spies to randomly patrol dressing rooms with calipers, tape measures and an eye for dirty tricks.) In addition, goalies may play the puck behind the goal line (which was also moved back six inches), only in a trapezoid-shaped area defined by lines that begin six feet from either goalpost and extend diagonally to points 28 feet apart at the end boards.

problem of why scoring is down in the NHL. Let's start with all of the clutching and grabbing and physical play on these small sheets of ice. The new rule changes will help somewhat in those areas, but the bottom line for the NHL was to open up scoring. So, the goalies are going to be lit up like they have never been before when it is all said and done. I am just glad they didn't make the nets bigger, which at one point was an option for them. That would have been a disaster.

You know, goalies are always outnumbered on a team 18-2 and with odds like that they lose every time. It is rare that they will listen to you in that environment, which can be really frustrating. Even now, with the lockout, who did they pick on? The goalies. Whose fault is it that the league is in disarray and why we are in this situation? Obviously, the goalies... I mean come on! That is so ridiculous, but what are goalies going to say, they are outnumbered a million to one out there and simply do not have a say in this stuff.

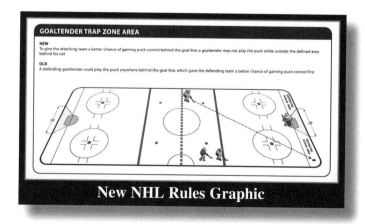

New NHL Rules Graphic

Apparently nobody appreciates a great defense anymore. The league wants more scoring and guess what? They are going to get it in a big way. I suppose that is what sells tickets these days. The other stuff, like the shoot-outs and getting rid of the red line, that is all good by me. I just thought that they really came down hard on the goalies because, of course, that is the path of least resistance.

Goalies are tough though and they too will persevere. Look at the numbers on this stuff and you will see that they need more help than just shrinking goalie pads. The shots on goal numbers in an average NHL game are way down. Go back 10-15 years ago and look at how many shots on goal an average game had, probably over 30. Today it is around 20-22. I am sorry, but the fact that goalies are getting 30-40% fewer shots on goal means that there are a lot of other issues going on in the game with regards to why scoring is down. It is not just because the pads have gotten bigger and more protective. Goal scoring is at a 50-year low (5.14 goals per game) and that is why they are calling this the "dead-puck era." The Goals Against (GA) average today is around 1.8 and that number is down from 2.8 a decade ago. It used to be a 3.0 GA was a great number, not anymore. Save percentages are up too. Great numbers used to range from 90-91% and now they are around 93-94%.

Another thing that drives me crazy is how they determine what a shot on goal actually is. That might be the most inefficient stat that there is. I mean it fluctuates from arena to arena without any consistency whatsoever. Some stat guys count a shot on goal as a shot from the other end, while others don't. It is archaic. So, until they can come up with a standardized system for that, we will never be able to really make sense of those numbers. Hey, it is not like a defenseman's plus-minus rating, which is pretty cut and dry. The shots on goal category is so vague and has a lot of room for interpretation. As a result it effects a lot of the scoring numbers that everybody is so up in arms about. Hey, why not use tape review to determine shots on goal or not? The goalies would all go for that so why not?

One last thing regarding equipment that nobody seems to be talking about are the new one-piece carbon fiber composite hockey sticks that give the shooters an extra 10% on their shots. The goalies need the added protection or they are going to get seriously injured at some point. Frozen vulcanized rubber traveling that fast tends to leave a tad bit more than just a mark. Multiply that repeated impact over all the practices and games over a season and we are talking about some serious bruising. Again, no problem for equipment improvements for the offensive guys, but as soon as they realize the goalies are also looking for an edge, they go ballistic. Whatever!

Look, goalies have gotten better. Much better. They player smarter, more efficiently and are a lot quicker. Moreover, they have grown exponentially over the past couple of decades. Did you know that in 1983 the average NHL goalie stood 5 feet 10 and weighed 179 pounds compared to six-foot and 191 pounds last season? Or, how about Washington Capitals behemoth Olaf Kolzig, who goes six-foot-three and 225, now that guy fills the net! So, to punish them for having gotten better is ridiculous in my opinion, but that is ultimately what they are going to do. We will just have to work that much harder, that's all. Goalies are just going to have to accept this and deal with it. Things will probably never change in that regard, so we will just have to make the best of it. At the Goalcrase we will prepare for it and train our kids accordingly.

ON BEING MARRIED TO A GOALIE...

I spoke of what it is like to be the parents of a goaltender, now I would like to speak a little bit about what it is like to be married to a goaltender. Obviously, if this is relevant for you, your husband will be in at least the college ranks and probably the professional ranks. Pro hockey does not necessarily mean the NHL either, in fact there are a boat load more opportunities for guys to play pro hockey either in the minor leagues or else over in Europe.

Here is the deal. A lot of goalies in professional hockey have a hard time with their marriages. For instance, my ex-wife couldn't handle being a "goalie wife." It is a tough, tough position to be in, no question. Just like some moms can't stand the pressure, the ridiculing and the intensity of it all, such is the case for a lot of wives and girlfriends of goaltenders. It broke my heart to see my ex-wife coming out of the rink crying. Seeing people boo me, say terrible things about me and even throw things down at the ice towards me — it all got to be too much for her. Fans can be so brutal, but that is just a part of the game at that level. It is an ugly part of the game, but a part of it nonetheless.

The tough part for me was that she would take that frustration, anxiety and fear home with her. That is where it really hurt. For me, I was used to all of that stuff. As a goalie you grow up with it and learn to channel it out and to just focus on the game. Well, for a wife to have to sit through that is a lot to ask sometimes. They tend take it personally, like any other rational person. Some women can deal with it and others can't. You just never know. Well, for me, to come home after a tough loss and then have to deal with everything all over again with her, that was so tough. Again, I learned long ago to leave my emotions at the rink, otherwise it can consume your entire life. So, that was frustrating.

Sometimes she even used to get sucked into arguments up in the stands trying to defend me if I let a goal in or something. This stuff didn't just happen at road games either, your home town fans can be your worst critics sometimes, believe me. I, of course, was oblivious to this down on the ice, but would hear about it when I got home. It is hard to talk rationally to a bunch of fans who have paid a high price for their tickets and want to express themselves. But hey, that is a side of goaltending that has existed for a long, long time.

The moral of the story is that you better have thick skin to play this position, and it helps if your significant other does too. Dealing with this stuff was very unhealthy for our marriage and was ultimately one of the reasons why we split up. At that level, you also have to be careful about bringing your kids out to see you as well. Again, anybody playing pro hockey that has kids old enough to go to games is probably doing OK for themselves, but it is tough to insulate them from all of those things. Just be careful and try to handle each situation as it presents itself.

Here are some thoughts and insights from my ex-wife, Alison, which I thought were pretty poignant:

ON THE PERILS OF BEING AN NHL GOALIE WIFE...

"It is a lot like being the wife of an NFL kicker, your husband is either the hero or the goat and there is not much room in the middle," said Alison. "It is just tough to be the wife of a professional athlete, period. But, to be the wife of a player who is constantly under so much pressure and so much stress, well that is even tougher I think. I remember when Robb was playing with the L.A. Kings, management would put all of the wives together to sit in the same section. Well, everybody except for me that was. Yeah, it was incredible! The goalie wife had to sit on the opposite side of the rink all by herself. I couldn't believe it. I mean you always hear about how goalies are so lonely and isolated, well I can officially say that their wives are too! I actually enjoyed it even more though because I could be alone and didn't have to listen to them whine about Robb when he let a goal in or did something wrong. Don't get me wrong, none of the wives were ever mean or anything like that, it was just a difficult situation to be in sometimes. I just got so nervous up there that it was nice to just be alone, otherwise I was a wreck — especially in overtime games and stuff like that. Plus, I got to sit down closer to the ice, which was great because for two periods I was right behind him and could be really close to him. I even caught a puck that he deflected off his stick one time, how cool is that? I remember another time during the Stanley Cup Finals out in L.A. where I had Robb's parents sitting on either side of me just grabbing onto my thighs in sheer terror. They were so nervous it was insane. Robb's dad was out pacing in the halls half the time while his mom and I were clutching each other back at the seats. It is a real trip to be under that much stress, but it is also one of the most exciting things in the world too."

ON DEALING WITH THE STRESS...

"I ran track and cross country at the University of Minnesota, so I understand what it is like to be an athlete performing at a high level and how to deal with pressure. Running is an individual sport, however, and you could control your own destiny, not like goaltending. So, for me to be on that side of the fence was nerve-racking to say the least. I felt so out of control sitting in the stands and it was just very stressful for me. What goalies have to go through is incredible. I don't know how they do it to tell you the truth. I remember sitting in the stands during games when Robb was playing in the NHL and hearing the fans say the most horrible things you could imagine — right in front of me. It was so hard. If the team is losing and not playing well the fans feel like they have the right to just say whatever they want to in order to make themselves feel better. I couldn't believe the things some of these idiots would say right to my face. It was never ever easy to be the wife of the goaltender, never. The stress came home from the rink and followed you around everywhere, it was very difficult to deal with quite honestly."

ADVICE FOR PARENTS & SIGNIFICANT OTHERS...

"The best advice I have for parents or spouses of goaltenders is to just go to the games and try to enjoy yourselves. Whatever you do, don't listen to the people around you. That is really hard to do, but you have to just tune them out. Otherwise you will go crazy listening to all of the bad things people say. It's like every time a goal is scored they are upset at the goalie, I mean come on! It is crazy sometimes. Most fans simply don't understand the nuances of goaltending the way the families of goaltenders do. They just bitch about the bad stuff and complain when things are going bad. Sure, they cheer when things are going great, but even during a close game they can be cruel without even realizing what they are doing. So, when you do hear things, you have to remember that most fans just don't understand what goalies go through and that they probably never will. They will never have that connection. Let their ignorance roll off your back or else you will go nuts.

"Beyond that, always remember to be as supportive as possible of your goalie. Give them a hug after the game, win or lose, and let them know that you are there for them. It is such an isolated position and oftentimes you might be the only person that they can talk to about things. They are really on an island a lot of the time. It is a very, very tough position. But, while it can be frustrating and lonely, it can also be the most glorious thing in the world as well. When you win a game and everybody comes down to jump on the goalie, that is the best. You have to savor those moments and remember them when things get bad — because they will turn eventually. Just try to keep it even by not letting the highs get too high or the lows get too low. If you are going to be in it for the long haul, like I was, then you have to know these things going in."

ON YOUR OWN KIDS PLAYING HOCKEY...

"Our kids Ruby and Jaxson are just five and six years old and I am aware that some day they may feel pressure to play hockey just because of their last name. So, we skate with them and have fun, but we really don't have them training to be goaltenders or anything like that at this point. If they want to play, then that is great, but we are not overloading them with any of that at all. We just want them to like sports and do things in moderation. I have always been fearful of them feeling like there would be too much emphasis on hockey in their lives, so that is why we have taken that approach with them. They enjoy going to the Goalcrease with their dad, and that is great, but we are definitely not that into it as of yet. We enrolled them this past year in a pond hockey program in Wayzata, but it was nothing major — just for fun. I mean Jaxson laid on the ice and made snow angels half the time! So, we will keep it all in perspective as time goes by. Even though Robb and I are no longer together, we both want what is best for the kids. We will always have that in common."

ON ROBB'S UNIQUE STYLE IN GOAL...

"One thing I will say about Robb was that when he was back in net, it was always going to be an adventure because you never knew what was going to happen. The fans loved that about him, he was so exciting as a player. You just never knew what he would do next and that never made for a dull moment with him out on the ice. He added so much to the game and was so entertaining to watch. He truly made games fun, that was for sure. He could always turn it on and turn it off too, which amazed me. He could have a terrible game and then come home like nothing happened. I couldn't do that. It stuck with me and just lingered. I guess that was why he was so good, because he could focus on what was happening and then let it go in order to get ready for his next game.

"I remember a funny story one time when he was playing with the Buffalo Sabres and he got sent down to the minors in Rochester. Well, he was going to go on a super long road trip so I went back home to Minnesota to see my family. Anyway, he calls me one night before a game and I told him that I missed him and that I wanted him to do something special for me that night. I always gave him little pep talks before his games but on that particular night for whatever reason I said, 'You gotta score a goal tonight...' He's like 'Yeah, whatever...' Well, sure enough, I get a call after the game and he is so excited he can hardly speak. I am like 'What, what happened?' 'What did you ask me to do before the game,' he said. 'No way,' I said, but sure enough, he did it. He scored his first goal. I couldn't believe it. He's like 'Quick, turn on ESPN, I am the Play of the Day!' That was awesome, I will never forget that."

ON ROBB AND THE GOALCREASE...

"Robb is just excellent with the kids and he has a real passion for what he does. He cares about young people and genuinely wants them to succeed. His knowledge of the game is so good and it is neat for him to be able to have a place where he can use that to make others better. His approach is very different from other coaches and he takes it all very seriously. He knows that goaltenders need that extra attention and he gives it to them. He goes so far beyond just teaching kids about how to make simple saves as goalies. He teaches them about other things such as nutrition, the benefits of physical fit-

THE COMEBACK KID?

Did you know that in 2003 & 2004 Robb signed a couple of two-day contracts to play down in the Atlantic Coast Hockey League & WH2 with the Jacksonville Barracudas? That's right. The team, which is coached by former NHL star Ron Duguay and Robb's former Gopher teammate, Bret Strot, thought it would be fun to get their old buddy back  onto the ice, and he jumped at the opportunity to lace em' up again. Staub's played great too, winning a pair and losing a pair to go .500 and proving that even as an old man — he's still got it!

ness, the importance of doing well in school, and about having a positive attitude. He knows that all of those things go into building self confidence and self esteem, qualities which transcend sports into real life. Robb is a thinker and doesn't say things that he doesn't mean. He is a man of few words, but when he does speak it is usually right to the point.

"As for the Goalcrease itself, Robb has made it a family environment there and has really taken into consideration the role of the parents. I mean there are a lot of things to do there for the parents and as a result, they enjoy coming there with their kids. It is a fun place that is for sure. Being a goalie is a very unique thing and having the Goalcrease is a wonderful thing for them. So, I am happy to see Robb living his dream and giving back to others at the same time, it is a great thing. Even though I am the ex-wife, I am very, very proud of Robb. He is so passionate about what he does and it is wonderful to see him in his element. This is truly his calling. When he retired from pro hockey he struggled with what he wanted to do, but now, after all these years it is great to see him doing what he loves and to be having so much success. He is a great motivator, a great speaker and a great coach. So, this is really a dream come true for him."

Paul Ostby & Robb go way back to their days as Gophers

CHAPTER EIGHT:
SOME WORLDLY ADVICE FOR GOALIES OF ALL AGES

ON WORK ETHIC...

The best way to establish a great rapport with your teammates is to never give up. Period. You have to earn your teammates' respect and the fastest way to do that is to try your hardest and never quit on a play. If guys see you playing emotionally then that is contagious. I mean there might be times when you get burned pretty badly on a play, but if you at least dive and show an effort to be competitive, then your teammates will see that you are trying. If you give up on it and just let the puck go in uncontested, you are going to lose their respect big-time. Plus, the coach might yank you at that point as well. Just never give up on a play, ever. That starts in practice too, where you build your confidence and establish your work ethic. I always tell young goaltenders that it is so important to compete in practice. You have to make it hard for them to score on you. Your teammates want that and they need that to get better. You will be letting your team down if you loaf in practice and that can be detrimental. Stuff like that can carry over to a game and then you are done for.

As a goalie you are the quarterback out there, directing traffic and leading by example. It is your job to help make your teammates to become better. Absolutely try to stop everything in practice and don't let pucks in the net unless they deserve to be in there. No soft goals. Now, if it has been a long practice and you are about to see your 750th shot of the afternoon, then maybe take every second or third shot real seriously. Make it obvious as to what you are doing though and guys will understand at that point. You can't go that hard for that long without getting completely spent, which could also lead to an injury too. So, play it by ear but remember to try hard all the time.

ON TRAINING PROPERLY...

Now that I have been teaching and coaching for a while I have seen quite a few things that really intrigue me. One thing in particular that I see every year is an onslaught of phone calls every August and September from parents who want to get their kids in to do some quick training for try-outs. "We want to get our son to see you so he will make the A team, or the B team, or the traveling team..." I hear this all the time and I have to sort of chuckle. The reality is that this stuff doesn't happen overnight. To try to cram it all in in order to make an A team is really sort of ridiculous. It's like opening the book for the first time to cram for a final exam in college the night before the test. It doesn't work. You need to start training in May or June to get ready. And that doesn't mean playing hockey every day either. That means getting in shape, eating right, doing dry land training and being mentally prepared. Remember, you are going to be tested and judged in your tryout on a lot of things besides how well you can stop a puck.

Then, when you finally do make that A team, don't slack off once you get there. I see that a lot, where kids will work hard to make a team and then relax, thinking they are set. When they have to stop working hard, they go backwards in their development. I think that for a lot of kids it seems like making an A team is just a short term goal. A lot of times that goal is driven by the parent too, which can also be bad.

The bottom line here is that you have to remember that being a good goaltender takes time. Period. It is a long process and each step along the way is all a part of the journey. What we like to do with young kids is set them up on a long-term program, complete with a lot of reachable and attainable goals. We want to maximize their skill and potential, that is key. In order to do that however, you have to be committed and you have to work very hard in order to succeed. You also have to be patient, because it all takes time. Big results don't happen in a month, they happen over the course of a season and into the ensuing off-season. We give kids a plan and then work with them to achieve their goals within that plan. We also try to work with the parents as well, to include them in the plan as much as possible. Being a goalie is a team effort and again, that starts at home. We are very consistent in our approach and that is what being a goalie is all about, consistency.

ON ESTABLISHING YOUR OWN STYLE...

Sometimes when I hear kids talking about their "style," I have to chuckle. When a 15 year old kid comes up to me and tells me he has a style, I tell him that he doesn't have a clue what a style is yet. Hey, you've been playing for eight years and you already have a style? I don't think so. When you are 24 or 25 and have been around the block a few times, then you can say you have a style. Kids just hear things, like they need to have a style, and then they try to emulate whatever that is. This can be really bad. You just have to let yourself grow and become a well rounded goaltender. That can be tough, to learn new styles and open yourself up to failure. Remember though, allowing yourself to fail is not only OK, it is vital to learning and mastering a new move. If you don't do that, then you will allow yourself to revert back to your old moves because they feel safer and more comfortable. Failure in goaltending is a part of life. So many goalies want to stop every shot, which is great because they are competitive, but it is really unrealistic. Sure, if you are getting beat in a certain area then you need to make adjustments. And, with those adjustments might come a new move. Then, when you are mastering a new move, remember, you will have set-backs and failures because those things take time. That is OK as long as you are learning and trying to get better.

Embrace it, you are growing as a goalie and taking steps to better yourself, that is all good.

Another bit of advice I have for young goalies is for them to go out and watch as many good goalies play as possible. Whether that is at your high school or at a college game or an NHL game, it doesn't matter. Learn as much as you can from guys better than you. Watch it on TV too. If an NHL game is on, watch it and study the goaltenders on each end. If your parents don't have ESPN, then beg and plead them to get cable so that you can watch games during the season. Beyond that, try to go to a college practice if you can and really watch to see what is going on. Visualize yourself in net and ask yourself what you would do in each situation. That is how you are going to get better. Watch that goalies' footwork; watch him play the angles; study his move selection; watch him steer pucks away and pass pucks up to his forwards to start an offensive break-out. There are so many things you can watch for; just soak it in and learn as much as possible.

FOOTWORK, FOOTWORK, FOOTWORK...

Footwork is the first thing I look for when I am evaluating a goaltender. Does he or she have clean footwork? How strong are they on their edges? Do you they have a good basic stance? Can they move laterally? Are they efficient? Are they in control of their body and do they have it in a nice compact position? How well do they move around their crease? That is where it all starts from, your footwork, and it affects everything else from the bottom up. Without good footwork you can't be in position to play the proper angles, then you are flopping around on your stomach diving for pucks. You may get lucky doing this, but over the course of a season you will fail much more than you succeed, guaranteed.

The bottom line is that the goalies who are smooth and make the game look easy are the ones who are going to succeed the most. They are the ones on the traveling team; they are the ones on the A team; they are the ones on the varsity; they are the ones playing Junior A; they are the ones getting the college scholarships; and they are the ones who eventually wind up playing professional hockey. It is safe to say that if you are diving around and are out of position, then you can usually assume that you have done something wrong. It doesn't matter if you are a great athlete and can dive for pucks all afternoon, nothing can take the place of a disciplined goalie who knows the angles and makes the correct save selections. Oftentimes when a goalie has a great game it is because he didn't dive around. If you are in perfect position all game then pucks just hit you and bounce off of you. That is when a goalie is in the zone and playing good, clean hockey.

Now, ESPN won't show highlights of a goalie playing perfect position and executing solid footwork. They will only show the sprawling, diving, sliding, acrobatic stuff that makes the crowd go ooh and aah. Sure, that is fun, and great goalies definitely make great saves, but it is the consistent fundamentals that matter most at the end of the day. The fact of the matter is that by the time a goaltender has to dive to make a great save, he was probably overcompensating for being so far out of position. So, it's OK for kids to emulate that, as long as they use that move as a last resort if they know that they are going to get beat.

ON DEALING WITH ADVERSITY...

I think that overall you have to try to be positive and just work hard. I don't care if you are Wayne Gretzky or Patrick Roy, everybody goes through ups and downs in their career. It is how you react to those adverse situations and what you make of them that matters. Everyone goes through adversity, but good players find ways to come out on top. You can either meet those challenges and accept them, or you are not going to make it. I mean we have all been on the short side of the stick at some point in our lives and we just have to get up and try harder the next time. I deal with parents all the time who complain to me that their kids have gotten a raw deal and that their coach doesn't like them or this or that. All I can say is "Guess what, who hasn't?" Every kid goes through that stuff, it is what you as a strong person do about it that matters. Are you going to dig your heels in and compete or pack it in and fold the tent? Those types of things are character builders in my opinion and it is all part of life. It might not be fair or fun, but it is reality and it is how you deal with adversity that helps you grow as an individual. Look, you are not going to play well or win every game, that is impossible. Don't ever forget that. Playing goaltender is a marathon not a sprint, and that is why we play for an entire season — so we can learn and get better as we go. Stay strong physically and stay strong mentally and you will be OK in the long run.

ON INTIMIDATION...

Personally, I think it is dumb to clear guys out of the crease for no good reason. Choose your battles wisely. I mean why would you want to wake up the other team and give them a reason to get fired up? It makes no sense. Players who sit on the door step and hack at you know that they have a role to play. I understood that. I also understood that if I was whacking them back, then I would not be very focused on my job — which is first and foremost to stop the puck from entering the net. It is tough to concentrate though when there is a guy parked out front and trying to screen you. Because then you have to have one of your defensemen come over and physically remove him, which makes for even more traffic out front. Before long you are just blinded with bodies and are very vulnerable. Plus, the odds of a deflection go way up at that point as well. So, you have to just deal with those distractions and try not to let them get to you too much. Other teams will watch you to see what you do in that situation. I mean if they put someone in front to mess with your head and you respond by freaking out and trying to whack the guy out of there, they will leave him there all game because they know he will mess with your concentration. Congratulations, you just made your job that much tougher.

I tried to ignore that stuff and felt it was always better to be quiet and let the preverbal "sleeping giant" lie. My crease was my sanctuary and the last thing I wanted was some idiot hanging out in there making my life miserable. Some guys dealt with it better than others I think. I mean you had some guys like Billy Smith, the great New York Islanders goalie of the early '80s, who used to just beat the crap out of guys who came into his crease. That was his strategy and guys used to fear him. He would butt-end guys with his stick and make them pay a price for being there. Philadelphia's Ron Hextall was another guy like that who ultimately had to change his ways too. That was there team's M.O., to be the "Broad Street Bullies," and not take any crap from anybody. If you messed with them, then they were going to fight you. It was a strategy that worked for them because they had the big guys who could back it up. Teams used to hate to play there because they knew they were going to have to play physical night in and night out. A lot of players used to mysteriously come down with cases of the *"Philly-Flu"* the night before games there, because they did not want to get beat up.

Other guys, like Vancouver goalie Dan Cloutier, who I played with in the minors, had to change his game completely. He used to get so worked up out there and just go ape when guys hacked at his stick and messed with him. Well, other teams picked up on that and really went after him hard to get him flustered. So, he had to change his whole philosophy in order to stay effective. Teams would just park a goon out front and that guy would hack him and talk to him to get him thinking about him and not the puck. To be honest, it is a good tactic. Trust me, it is hard enough to concentrate on a 95 mph puck coming at your head without having to worry about what a guy is saying about your mother right next to you.

There are a lot of ways to "own your crease," but hacking guys to clear them out is definitely something that has consequences. But, if you are in a game where you are down 6-1, then sending the other team a clear message might be an appropriate thing to do. Pure frustration might outweigh common sense at that point. The bottom line is that you are sort of damned if you do and damned if you don't, so take it on a game by game basis as to how you want to deal with those people. You don't want to invite them over and let them get too cozy, but at the same time you have to send them a message that they are not welcome in your crease. If you are so focused and consistent on what is happening in front of you, then that is only going to invite more problems. You have to find a balance out there and let's face it, that may require a few love-pats to the back of a few ankles in order to get your point across.

"Lindsay has been going to the Goalcrease for a few years now and she just loves it. As a parent, we have been really happy with Robb and the entire staff over there. They do a great job and it has definitely been money well spent for us. Prior to Robb coming in there was only goalie instruction offered in the Summer around here, so we have enjoyed seeing Lindsay progress throughout the season, when it matters most. Lindsay has been to other camps in the area, but none of them offer year round training. Logistically, I love being able to schedule her appointments at my convenience and around my own schedule. The flexibility is fabulous. Beyond that, she loves the one-on-one instruction that she gets. That has made the biggest impact on her development I think. The videotape analysis is also very helpful too, so that she can see where she needs to improve on things.

"She enjoys working with Robb and Laura, and also with Clint and Jeff too. All of the people are so dedicated there. Each instructor brings something different to the mix and the kids seem to enjoy that variety. All of them have the same principles though and the consistency is always there. Each kid gets their own personalized program and that is so nice to see. The repetitiveness is the key. They work with her on something until she gets it right. They also keep detailed notes about her sessions and then they pick up where they left off the next time she comes in. They just prepare her very well and that shows in her development. Her fundamentals have gotten much better and as a result, she is having a lot more fun playing the game.

"Whenever Lindsay walks in they all know her by name and they immediately want to know what she has been up to. Robb will come over and show her how to tape a stick properly and just do a lot of little things that make a difference. She loves it. It is a wonderful atmosphere there. The Goalcrease is more expensive than the other camps around the area but it is by far and away the best of the best. It is totally worth it and that is why we will keep going back in the future. It is a great investment in our daughter's future and you really do get what you pay for.

"The role modeling there is great too. All of the instructors played at a high level and they have a lot of credibility in terms of what they are talking about. I remember one time the goalie from the Harvard women's team was there and Lindsay got to not only meet her and talk to her, but she also got to go through her drills as well. It was such a neat experience for her. It is also so great to have so many opportunities for girls in general. Most other places are so centered around the boys, but the Goalcrease has just as many programs for the girls and that is nice.

"She has improved so much since she started going there and her con-

fidence is way up too. Lindsay's goals are to play on the varsity and then play in college. So, I am sure that if she keeps up the hard work and continues to train at the Goalcrease then the sky is the limit for her. Their program is just totally unique and as parents we couldn't be more pleased with the entire package. To have Robb and the Goalcrease here, locally, is just a gold mine."
— Julie Brown, Daughter Lindsay Plays U-12 in the Irondale Association

"The Goalcrease is awesome. I always look forward to coming there because all of the coaches are so nice. They talk to you and crack a lot of jokes and stuff, it is really fun. I also like how they do one on one training with us. There is nobody else around when they are training you and that makes you feel really special. All of their attention is focused on you and that motivates you to listen better and to try and get whatever they are trying to teach you. I think I have improved a lot over the past couple of years that I have been going there. For instance, my glove and blocker are way better. Before I got there I wasn't very coordinated with them, but now I really like using them. I have also really gotten better with my stick. My stick saves are a lot better and I have lot more confidence to use it. When I was playing U-10 I was horrible. But since I started seeing Robb my stats in U-12 have gotten way better. I also think that using the Staubar helped me a lot too. At first I didn't like using it, but then when I got the hang of it, it helped me a lot. Beyond that, they just got me out of my bad habits and that has really made a difference too. It's just a great place to come to learn about hockey." **— Lindsay Brown, Plays U-12 in the Irondale Association**

"I think Robb runs just a top-flight program and he has been very helpful and instrumental in Lindsay's development. She has really enjoyed her time at the Goalcrease and it has certainly made a difference in her play. Her time there has helped her immensely in terms of her confidence and in terms of her knowledge of the game. They have really taught her the mechanics well, from the angles to footwork, she has learned a great deal from them. I think Whitney makes almost all of her first saves in our games, but then it becomes a rebound issue out front — which is always an adventure with kids that age. So, she has a lot of work to do but we know that she is in great hands over at the Goalcrease. She has really blossomed as not only a goalie but as an athlete, and I attribute a lot of that success to Robb and his staff.

"For me, as a coach, it was so nice to know that a trained professional was teaching my goaltender. I mean the extent of my goalie coaching expertise consists of a few key phrases: "Stop it!", "Go down!", "Don't go down!", and "Freeze the thing!". So, obviously we were all pleased when she started learning from the pros. He has helped our entire youth hockey association immensely by getting us all on the same page and by working closely with our goaltenders to get them better. All of the staff at the Goalcrease are great and they all stress the fundamentals in a way that encourages the kids to do their best. They videotape the kids and then give them outstanding feedback afterwards, which is so nice to see. You get a lot of one-on-one training there and even a good deal of two-on-one training, which is almost unheard of these days. Plus, the facility is absolutely top notch, a real goalie heaven.

She really enjoys working with Jeff, Clint and Laura, and has so much fun taking lessons from them. All of the instructors coach the same things and share the same philosophies, but each one has a different style and individual personality. So, the variety of coaches makes it nice for the kids I think. They have a great camp, they are great people, they have interesting and refreshing perspectives on the game and that is why they are the best in the business. It is expensive but it is worth it. Robb is a real Zen-master and our entire association is grateful to have found him." — **Whitney Johnson, Coaches Lindsay's U-12 A-Team in the Irondale Association**

****

"Our experience with the Goalcrease has been fabulous. I love the individualized attention my daughter gets there and most importantly, she has fun when she's there. She really likes the instructors too, they are all so nice. She had never gotten any coaching before because none of the coaches on her team knew very much about goaltending. So, she would just block shots all day in practice while the other kids did drills and then play in games, never really learning anything to get better. That was very frustrating to see her trying hard but knowing that she wasn't getting any instruction specifically for goalies. Since we have been coming to Robb though, her game has improved drastically. They are strictly goalie experts and that is so refreshing to see as a parent of a young goaltender. Rebecca first met Robb when he was doing clinics and then when he opened the Goalcrease, she was one of the first kids to sign up. She has been going ever since and just loves it. People tell me she has a lot of talent, so for her to get the training she deserves makes me feel good as a mom." — **Connie Macrostie, Daughter Rebecca is 15 and plays for a CO-OP Team in the Twin Cities District of St. Paul**

"Going to the Goalcrease is a lot of fun. I go year round and I learn so much, it is awesome. We have our own girls locker-room and the place is super nice. The instructors are fun and really nice too. And, they all are really good goalies so I learn a lot from them. I have gotten a lot better since I have been going there the past few years and I definitely make more saves for my team when I am out on the ice. All of my coaches have told me that I have improved too, which makes me happy. They are glad that I go there because they don't know a lot about coaching goaltenders. So, that is great. Robb really taught me a lot about angles and about being in the right place at the right time. He also explained to me when it was good to go down and when to stay up, stuff like that. Then, when he videotapes us, we can see where we are making mistakes. He is real positive too, which is nice. I just really like going there, it is always a good experience for me." — **Rebecca Macrostie is 15 and plays for a CO-OP Team in the Twin Cities District of St. Paul**

****

"Let me preface my comments by saying that I played D-I hockey at Providence back in the early 70s and a little bit of pro over in Europe too. In addition, I have coached for several years at the youth level as well. So, I say this as a parent who has a pretty good hockey background and hopefully a little bit of credibility. Having said that, I would just like to say that over the past three years the I have known Robb I can't think of a person who has better talent in coaching kids than him. It is not just goaltending either. He teaches them about the entire game as well as about the mental side of it too. He is the most positive influence on these kids and I honestly can't say enough good things about him. He has such a passion to teach goaltending and the kids just love him.

"He has so much credibility with them too. I mean as a former NHLer he is such a gifted athlete and has such outstanding hand-eye coordination. So, when he demonstrates a move, you can just see the kids go 'Wow!'. That is what is so unique about Robb. You know, there are very few people where things come so easy to who can relate to others so well. I mean typically the greatest athletes are not the greatest coaches. Robb bridges that gap better than anybody.

"You know, there is a saying in business that goes "Money buys but enthusiasm sells...", and that is Robb to a tee. He is constantly looking to develop the best possible move for the most appropriate situation. He's not trying to make them "Stauber goalies," he is trying to get them to be the best that they can be. He focuses on about a half a dozen basic moves that are absolutely necessary to become a good goaltender and he's always working on the best ways to teach and implement those moves. I am just really impressed with the guy.

"My daughter was invited to one of his PUSH program's last year where he invited just six top level goalies out and it was amazing. He worked them so hard both on and off the ice that they could hardly move the next day. If the kids are serious about getting better, then there is no better place to go than the Goalcrease. You can sit behind the glass at the Goalcrease with the other parents and listen to them all rave about Robb and what a great person he is. Robb's competitors have advertised against him and because he is such a nice guy he doesn't want to go after them. It doesn't matter though because every parent I have ever talked to says that the other guys don't even come close to the Goalcrease. Once he gets kids in the door, there is just no question that they are in the best possible place for the development of goaltending.

"My daughter probably would not even be playing hockey today without Robb, no way. Despite the fact that she is only four-foot-ten and just 85 pounds, he has made her so technically sound it is unbelievable. I mean she doesn't fill up any net so she has to compensate with superior fundamentals. So, Robb just focused on her angles and her footwork to compensate for her lack of size. Mentally and physically it is like night and day since she started coming to the Goalcrease. And her confidence is so strong now too.

Let me reiterate again, I have no vested interest in Robb or his business, so I say this from the heart as a very satisfied customer. He is just a great guy who can flat-out coach. Again, I played for some great Hall of Fame coaches along the way, guys like Dave Peterson and Lou Lamoriello, so it's not like I am just a guy off the street saying this about Robb. I really feel strongly about him and his program and am lucky to have my kid be a part of it. We really believe in this guy, he's a genius." — **Terry Nagle, Daughter Amanda plays for Benilde St. Margaret's High School**

"Robb is a great teacher and so funny. I can honestly say that he has taught me everything I know about goaltending. I have learned so much from him, especially things like never giving up and staying motivated. In the four years that I have seen Robb my game has completely changed, from the way I hold my stick, to my quickness, to the way I skate on my toes, he has just really helped me. He also got rid of all my bad habits too. Because I am so small he had me focus a lot on my stick work, like the rotation, so I can cover more space. Then, the Staubar helps me keep my arms where they should be and that covers up holes too. My game is so much better now and I just have a lot more confidence when I am out there. His personal stories really help me as well, like when he had to play as a back-up in the NHL. He just talked about staying positive and being patient. Well, when I had to play back-up last year, I thought about what he said and that really helped me get through it. As for my future, I am hoping to go on to play in college down the road and I know that if Robb continues to help me work on my game, then I have a good chance. I also want to say that I really like being around all of the people there, they are all so nice. I especially like working with Paul Ostby, who also coaches at Benilde St. Margaret's. He is a lot of fun to work with and really helps me too." — **Amanda Nagle, plays for Benilde St. Margaret's High School**

****

"My son has learned a great deal at the Goalcrease. Not only have they taught him a lot of things, they have also been a great support system for him. They have taught him both the physical as well as the mental sides of the game and it has been a real positive experience for him overall. He particularly likes the fact that everybody there is a former goaltender, so they understand exactly what is going on with everything. They speak a common language with the kids, so they can really relate to them on their own level. They use a lot of positive reinforcement too, which is great for their self confidence. They spend really quality time with the kids there, working on specific drills that will benefit them each individually. Videotaping is another thing he really likes because he can actually see what the problems are, versus a coach yelling at him about a play after the fact. Beyond that they just encourage them to work really hard and that there are no shortcuts. As a parent, when you can see your kid actually apply the same techniques during a game that he just learned at the academy, then you have to feel pretty good about what you are doing. Pete has aspirations to play at a higher level, whether that is at the junior level or college level will remain to be seen. Robb and Paul understand this and they work closely with him so that he can try to meet his goals. He definitely has an edge up over the other kids by going there and I can honestly say that it has been a great investment." — **Mike O'Hara, Son Pete Plays for Holy Angels High School**

"Mike has been seeing Robb for over five years now and he has really enjoyed his time with him at the Goalcrease. Robb teaches the basics first and then adds in so many other great techniques for the kids to learn. He and his staff are so knowledgeable and what I like most about them is that their messages have practical applications for everyday life. So, instead of coaching they are teaching, and I like that. I have noticed a big improvement in Mike since he has been going there. He is much more confident; he is very sound technically; and he has learned the values of discipline and preparation.

"Last year Mike was invited to one of Robb's PUSH programs with a few other select kids. It was really intense. The one thing I remembered most about it though was when my son told me that after one of the practices everybody sat around afterwards and talked about what other things they liked to do besides hockey. They talked about school, family and about life. That to me says that Robb understands the big picture and I think that is wonderful. He wants to develop them as young adults and as individuals, not just as hockey players, which is so important. Robb focuses on quality not quantity, and that is why he is so well respected in the hockey community. He is very picky about selecting his staff and that is why they have such good people there. They all really compliment each other too. Clint, for instance, will give you a different perspective than Paul or Jeff. They all have a different way of doing things, yet they work well as a team to teach kids the right way to play the position.

"Hey, we drive in from Andover, more than 45 minutes, once a week to come see Robb. We just believe in it that much. I wouldn't think of going anywhere else. We have been to other camps, such as Tretiak's and a few others, but I love Robb's well-rounded approach to teaching and that is why we haven't been anywhere since coming to him several years ago. A lot of other camps just run kids through stations out on the ice and they do drills all day. At the Goalcrease, however, it is broken down to a customized plan for each individual. Sure, there may be two or three goalies at a certain station, but it is really focused. The one-on-one time they give the kids there is just great.

"As for Robb as a teacher, I think he it just outstanding. Because he was so successful in college and in the pros, he brings a lot of credibility to the table. As a player he was always hungry to keep improving and to learn from his setbacks. He carries that same attitude today and wants to pass on what he has learned to these kids. He is more than just focused on whether or not the kids are just good goalies. He is very intense and he hates to lose. And, he always wants to put on an exceptional practice session for his clients day in and day out. We are lucky to have him, he is a super guy." — **Gary Shibrowski, Son Mike Plays Bantams in Andover**

"I love going to the Goalcrease, they teach you a lot of cool stuff. The people who work there try to get to know you and they figure out what you need. Then they help you with that stuff each time you come in. I've improved a lot over the past few years since I started going there. Mentally I am stronger and I have a lot more confidence. I know that I can play with older kids and that makes me feel really good. Robb is a good teacher and takes the time to work with you until you get it. He encourages me to be confident in my abilities and skills. He taught me that my feet are my base and everything starts there, which has helped me a lot. The Staubar helped me a lot too, especially with correct posture and with angles.

"Sometimes after practice we will all sit around and just talk about life, not hockey. That is pretty neat. We talk about how goaltending can help you in your everyday life and why hard work is so important. We learned that if you work hard for things then you are going to get breaks, so you have to keep pushing and pushing ahead. I play other sports too, football and lacrosse, and my time at the Goalcrease has helped me in those sports as well. The only bad thing about the Goalcrease for me is the 45 minute drive, other than that I love it. I intend to keep going through high school and hopefully beyond." — **Mike Shibrowski, Plays Bantams in Andover**

****

"I've been going to see Robb and Paul for a long, long time and I really like those guys. The Goalcrease has been great for me and I have learned a ton there over the years. It is always quality one-on-one time with the instructors and I think that is what I like the most about it. They stress making good saves, not great saves. And what I mean by that is that they focus on teaching us the fundamentals more so than they do on making flashy saves. They also emphasize movement and using your feet too, which is where it all starts. Overall, it is a great place to be if you are a goaltender and I am lucky that I have been able to be there for as long as I have." — **David Goullaud, Plays at Wayzata High School**

****

"I have been seeing Robb since I was in the eighth grade and I wouldn't trade it for the world. It is such a unique place, there is nothing like it anywhere else. They are amazing to work with, such good teachers. Nobody can come close to what they do there, they are all totally experts. It is like goalie heaven over there, it is awesome. They just work you and work you until you get it and then your confidence just soars. The entire experience has just had an immensely positive effect on my life.

"As I continued to go there throughout high school at Edina my game steadily got better and better. I went undefeated my junior year and only lost a couple of games as a senior, and that was a lot of fun. Definitely working with Robb got me a lot better. I wore the Staubar early on and even though I didn't like it at first because it felt so uncomfortable, I hung in there and it really helped me. Eventually you just got the feel of what it was supposed to do and then you didn't need it any more.

"Robb is really good at getting you not to think but to just react instead. That all happens through repetition. The biggest thing he helped me with by far though was my footwork. I have become so much quicker on my feet and that has made all the difference in the world to me. When you are quick on your feet you are just always in a good position to make saves. When you aren't, then you are diving all over the place making desperation saves. You are also going up and down to your knees a lot too, which tires you out much quicker.

"With Robb I know that if I work hard then my destiny is in my own hands. He convinced me to lose weight when I was younger and it paid off big time. He has also taught me so many little tricks about proper technique and that has been amazing too. He has us do drills that sometimes you don't even know why we are doing them, but then a light bulb goes off and you just get it. He knows so much about the game, he is a great teacher. He takes everything down to the bare essentials and makes goaltending not easier, but simpler. Robb is just that good and that knowledgeable that he instantly earns your respect. He is the best coach I have ever had, for sure." **— Eric Hylok, Plays at St. Olaf College**

****

"We had Robb and his guys come down to work with our goaltenders on and off during last season and it worked out really well for us. We don't have a full time goalie coach, so those guys would come down one at a time to teach our kids new training techniques. I was really happy with what they did. They all have a real passion for teaching and coaching and that was obvious with the way they treated our goalies. They worked really hard and made the most out of their time with us. All of the kids really liked them and they developed relationships with them too — which is important at that position to have that level of trust. So, all in all it was a good experience for us and it certainly helped us get better." **— Mark Carlson, Head Coach of the Cedar Rapids Rough Riders Junior A Hockey Team**

****

"Our experience at the Goalcrease has been wonderful. First of all, all of the coaches there are just great with the kids. They are great instructors and they really connect with the kids at their own level. Robb and Paul have a great staff and they are just so knowledgeable about goaltending. My son Sam has been with the Goalcrease for a couple of years now and he has really improved over that time. We moved here from Utah and we were just blown away when we heard about the facility. After spending a Summer with Robb, Sam moved from Peewee B-2 all the way up to Peewee A. That didn't happen by luck either, that was absolutely attributable to the techniques and training that they taught him.

"He went through the PUSH program this last year and that just did wonders for him. The videotaping and personal attention made a big difference in him understanding what he was doing both right and wrong. They also work a lot on the mental aspects of being a goaltender there as well. Overall, Robb is just a great instructor; he is super knowledgeable; and he can really explain the techniques which are so vital for success at this position. Whatever goalie he is working with he is very keen at being able to dissect what they are doing right, what they need to be doing better and what they are doing wrong. More importantly, he can verbalize all of that in a way that can be comprehended by kids." — **Tim Calahan, Son Sam Plays Bantams in Edina**

"I love going to the Goalcrease, it is a lot of fun. The people there are funny and nice. You learn so much when you are there too, which is the most important thing. Pretty much everything I know about goaltending is from Robb and his staff. They are amazing at what they do. They teach you how to make quick decisions and to get into position so that you can make easy saves instead of hard ones. While they are really good in teaching us about angles, footwork, and the physical parts of the game, I think the thing they are the best at is teaching the mental part of it. They talk to us a lot about having the right attitude and that has made a big difference for me. Clint and Andy are probably my favorite coaches to work with over there. They are super funny and even though they are my coaches it seems like they are my friends. Robb is great too. As a teacher he is easy to work with and is so smart. He is demanding but he knows a lot and sincerely wants to teach you so that you get better. I advanced up to the peewee A team last year and we won the state title, so that was awesome. I couldn't have done it without Robb either, no way. I have been to a lot of other goalie camps and nothing comes close to the Goalcrease." — **Sam Calahan, Plays Bantams in Edina**

****

"Parker has been going to the Goalcrease for over three years now and he loves it. It has helped him improve a great deal and that has been great to see. One of the things we have come to accept over the years is that for the most part coaches, and I mean no disrespect here, don't have a lot of time to work with goalies. They are busy working with the players and frankly probably don't know a whole lot about the position. So, they just sort of throw them in the net and let them take shots while the team is practicing. Because of that, we love the Goalcrease. Parker gets a lot of attention here from goalies who truly understand what he is going through. He likes the instructors and he has made a lot of good friends here too. It is just a really positive situation for him.

"Robb is very hard on Parker, but Parker likes to be challenged. He is tough and demanding but that is because he wants him to excel and do his best. So, Parker enjoys that and thinks a lot of Robb as a teacher. Personally, I think Robb is a perfectionist and has truly made an art out of his craft of teaching goaltending. He expects the kids to work hard and they have a lot of respect for him in return. Robb has found a great niche for himself and I am very fortunate that my son loves going there so much." — **Pete Plucinak, Son Parker Plays Bantams in Chaska**

"I really like to be worked hard and that is exactly what they do for me at the Goalcrease. It makes me feel like I am actually doing something rather than just standing around like we do sometimes during practices with my team. I have gotten a lot better since I started seeing Robb and I wouldn't trade it for anything. I have gotten a lot quicker; I have more stamina; I have more confidence; and I play my angles much better. Whenever I have a problem with something they always have a technique on how to fix it. It is awesome. The coaches there work on all sorts of different things with you and are always trying to teach you new things.

"I have gone to a lot of other camps and they always try to teach you a whole new style. I hated that. Robb just works with you and teaches you how to get into the right positions and how to work from within your own style. That is why I love going there so much, it is very comfortable to me. They make you feel good about what you are doing and that just boosts your confidence. They give you a ton of one-on-one time too, which is great. The instructors are all really smart as well. They actually listen to you and don't just interrupt you when you ask them a question. You feel important there and you learn pretty quickly that they want to help you get better. It is so cool to learn something at the Goalcrease and then actually do it in a game. That is a rush.

"As a teacher, Robb is great. He is very strict but he works really hard to make sure you get what he is teaching you. He wants you to be focused all the time and even stresses that we have eye contact with him all the time so that we are always working on our concentration. Stuff like that doesn't seem like it would help, but once you are in a game and start to think about it, you get totally focused and can concentrate on the game without any distractions."
— **Parker Plucinak, Plays Bantams in Chaska**

****

"David has been seeing Robb for nearly 10 years now, so he is practically like family. He is just a wonderful person and an outstanding coach. Robb and his staff are exactly the type of people who I want my son to model himself after. They are just quality individuals. David is unique in the sense that he plays hockey during the hockey season as well as in the Summer, but he also plays other sports during other times of the year. We think it is great that he is well rounded that way and Robb completely supports that too.

"Robb and Paul (Ostby) have worked with him for so long and they have been such a positive influence on him. He has learned so much from them and I think a lot of that has crossed over into his everyday life as well. They have not only taught him hockey skills, but also mental skills on how to be a better person. As a parent we think that is fabulous. They teach him about hard work, having a positive attitude and having fun. Those are things that don't just apply to hockey. It is so much more than just teaching them goalie skills over there and that is great to see. It is just a very impressive group over there and we have been extremely pleased with them." — **Susan Sund, Son David Plays for Eden Prairie High School**

"The Goalcrease has been awesome. It is so much fun and I love going there. They force you to get better through hard work and practice. They are big on muscle memory and learning through repetition. The Staubar, for instance, ingrained good muscle memory as to where your arms should be. Robb is big on teaching good habits and eliminating bad ones. As a teacher, Robb is by far the best one I have ever had in hockey. He will get on you when you are not working hard or doing your best, and then when you do something right you will know that too. Since coming to the Goalcrease everything has improved in my game: footwork, leg strength, angles, proper positioning, everything. His drills are great too, the U-Drill, Y-Drill, X-Drill, Box-Drill, Inverted V-Drill — they are all so beneficial to learning proper technique. The videotaping also helps a lot because you get to see the pucks from a totally different perspective. You can see where you have holes and where you need to improve your position. Overall, the Goalcrease has been great and I just feel really lucky to have been able to go there for as long as I have." — **David Sund, Plays for Eden Prairie High School**

****

"The Goalcrease has been just wonderful for our family. The kids love it and we couldn't be more pleased with the entire experience. We are nuts about Robb, we think the world of him. He is a great teacher and a great role model for young people, so that is why we send our kids to him. His intensity is very contagious and he has such an unbelievable focus. Yet, he teaches kids in a really fun and positive way. He has a very playful, puppy-like personality about him and I think that is why kids gravitate towards him. I would say he is very creative and innovative as a teacher too. Robb is also very drill oriented at his practices and that builds the kids' confidence through all of the repetition. He just has a gift with regards to how he teaches his techniques to the kids in a way that they can understand, regardless of what level they are at in hockey.

"My husband and I are very pleased with the Goalcrease and would highly recommend it. The people there are just outstanding teachers. We have even joked that if Robb and Paul taught basket weaving instead of hockey, we would probably send our kids to learn that from them too. They are just that good and really worth every penny. They are great mentors and we think our kids get so much more out of seeing them than just learning how to stop pucks. Their motivational techniques and personalities are such a breath of fresh air and that is what it is all about for us.

"Robb is like a dad to all the kids there and he genuinely cares about them — sometimes even too much. A funny incident happened one time when my son Max was in about ninth grade. I got a call one morning pretty early and it was Robb. He says "Pam, I just wanted to let you know that I was at the movies last night and I saw Max there with a bunch of girls." I said "Yeah, we knew he was out and it was OK with us." Robb then says, "Well, I just wanted you to know because I want to make sure that he doesn't get too distracted..." I thanked him and told him I appreciated his concern, but that it was fine with us for him to go out with his friends and have fun. We thought it was pretty funny, but that is the kind of guy Robb is. He truly wants the best for his kids and wants to make sure things are going well with them in their personal lives as well as in their hockey lives. He wasn't checking up on him or anything, he just wanted to make sure that his priorities were in line. We were actually really impressed that he called, it showed how much he cared. If there is ever a potential distraction for his goalies, he is on the phone right away.

"Max was the starter on the high school team and has college aspirations, so they work with him at a very advanced level to make him better. Bailey, meanwhile, had a knee injury last year and they worked with him on that as well, which was just wonderful to see. They knew exactly what they were doing and made sure that he wouldn't re-injure himself. Paul was especially good on working with him after that and that made us as parents feel great. Paul and Robb work so well together and make a wonderful team. They have very different coaching philosophies and really compliment each other nicely." — **Pam Dodds, Mother of Max and Bailey (Max Played for Eden Prairie High School & Bailey is a Peewee)**

"I have been seeing Robb since I was a little kid and he has always been there for me to help me achieve my goals. My big goal now is to play Division One hockey and hopefully that will come true too. He is a great teacher and I owe a lot of my success to him. He is super intense and has so much enthusiasm for the game. Whenever I see him it just motivates me to be my best. Robb is so knowledgeable about every aspect of the game. His methods on teaching technique are amazing. He can pinpoint the smallest thing that you might be doing wrong and then explain to you how to correct it. The videotaping helps a lot with that as well. He is also really good about working with you until you get something too. You can go to him with any questions or problems you have and he will work with you until you get it resolved. My game has gotten so much better since I started seeing him and I would have to say that I owe everything to him. I would also say that Paul has been awesome too. He has worked with me a lot over the years as well and he is a great teacher in his own right. All of the people at Goalcrease are really smart and they want to make you better. It is just a great place to go if you are a goalie, there is nothing else like it." — **Max Dodds, Played for Eden Prairie High School**

"I love going there, it is a lot of fun. It is pretty cool to learn stuff while you are having fun at the same time. Every time I go in I learn something new and then I use it at practice and in games. Robb is intense but he makes you want to try your hardest so that you get better. He is just a great teacher and I hope that I can keep going to the Goalcrease for as long as I play." — **Bailey Dodds, Plays Peewees in Eden Prairie**

****

"We originally got introduced to Robb when our youth association hired him to come out to Maple Grove and give clinics. We were so impressed that we decided to send our son Tony down the Goalcrease to work with him one-on-one. Robb is a fantastic instructor and does so much for the kids. He gives them so much instruction that their regular coaches could never dream of giving them. It has helped him a great deal and we are very happy with that. There are so many things that most coaches don't understand or pay attention to that Robb does and that gives the goalies a real boost of self confidence. I think his enthusiasm is contagious too. He is great with technique and instruction, but he is just as valuable in teaching the kids about the mental side of the position as well. He gives each kid so much attention and really wants to see them improve. All of the guys there are great, they are all wonderful instructors. It doesn't matter who you work with up there, whether it is Robb or Paul or Jeff or Clint or anybody else — they are all really good and they all know their stuff.

"We have been to several other camps in the area and to be honest, nothing comes close. They just spend so much time with each kid it is incredible. They track their progress on the computer and on videotape, which is really nice. They don't waste any time there either, they know what each kid needs to work on and they get right to business. They know their kids inside and out. It is not like a camp where you go for a week and they make it a social thing. This is all business. Sure, the kids have fun, but they are going there to learn and they know that. So, it has just been a real positive experience for us, that is for sure. The investment in our son has been invaluable and that is what is most important at the end of the day in my book." — **Rollie Renstrom, Son Tony Plays High School Hockey in Maple Grove**

"I really enjoy it over there. I think the biggest thing for me has been learning technique from Robb. He pushes you pretty hard and never lets you quit. I like that. They all just encourage me to be better in everything I do and I have gotten a lot better as a result. They give you so much one-on-one instruction there that you can't help but improve. It is just a lot of fun going there and that is what hockey should be." — **Tony Renstrom, Plays High School Hockey in Maple Grove**

****

"We have been seeing Robb for several years now and we have been extremely happy with him. All of the instructors at the Goalcrease have such a positive attitude with the kids and as parents that makes you feel very good. The instructors have all played the position and continue to play the position, so they truly are experts in what they do. Each one has their own area of expertise too, which gives the kids a nice variety every time they come in. They have built a lot of confidence in our son, J.T., by challenging him and encouraging him to do his best. When he goes into tryouts now he has so much confidence and the coaches pick up on that right away. J.T. tends to be lazy in practices, but not when he is at the Goalcrease. They get the best out of him and he has really improved because of that. They are also very good at finding his weaknesses and then teaching him how to fix them in a way that fits his specific personality traits. He will tell them what he needs to work on sometimes and they will spend an entire session doing that. I think they genuinely care about the kids there and that is why we have continued to go back. They treat each kid like they are the client and give them just outstanding instruction. J.T. enjoys it there and we feel like it is a very positive influence on his life. In fact, it might be the single most positive thing that I have ever seen happen for him. Words can't describe how I feel about it, tears just come to my eyes. It is wonderful." — **Ruby Woodward, Son J.T. Plays Bantams in Prior Lake**

"I really like going to the Goalcrease, it has helped me to improve a lot. I have fun when I am there and I really like the instructors too. When you learn a new move or technique there they go over it and over it until you get it. They are tough but they want you to learn so that you get better. My favorite part of it is the videotaping because you can see what you are doing right and wrong. I went to a lot of other camps before Robb, but since I started going there I stopped going to any other camps. He is the best." — **J.T. Woodward, Plays Bantams in Prior Lake**

****

"Joe just loves going there and we love it too. He has been going there for four or five years now and it has made such a difference in his game. As a parent, it is such a huge feeling of satisfaction when you see your son get worked out by one of the professionals at the Goalcrease. You watch him come off the ice tired, but well educated and ready to take on the world. The one-on-one training the kids get there is so overwhelming. It is truly unbelievable. They really care about the kids there.

"His coaches at high school know that he is being trained by a professional and they just let him do his own thing. If a coach asks him to do something a certain way he will respectfully tell them that his coaches at the Goalcrease taught him to do it a different way and that is the way he would prefer to do it. They are all OK with that because they know he is in the best hands possible. His confidence has consistently gotten better and his game has gotten much better as well.

"They just take really good care of him there. If his equipment breaks down, they fix it; if he needs special help in a certain area, they teach him; they just do whatever it takes to make the kids feel great about themselves. They are tough and demanding though, and they expect them to work extremely hard during their time there. So, it can be challenging for them, but if they want to learn and get ahead, there is no better place than the Goalcrease. It is just an outstanding organization from top to bottom, just outstanding. I am being very sincere when I tell you that Robb Stauber has done more for my family than he will ever know." — **Jeff Dawson, Son Joe Plays at Hill Murray High School**

"The Goalcrease is awesome. You get so much one-on-one instruction from the teachers over there, it is great. They push me really hard and I enjoy being challenged like that. Every time you get on the ice they challenge you and that makes you better. When you are tired and want to give up, they push you to dig deep and stay mentally tough. So, my stamina has totally improved because of that and I just feel more confident when I am playing in games. Robb is a great teacher. He is a disciplinarian yet he is also really fun too. He will let you goof around when you are off the ice, but as soon as your session starts he is all business. I respect that because I know that he wants to make me a better goalie. It is also neat to know that the instruction I am getting is the same as the pros in the NHL get. He has also taught me to be aggressive with the puck and to go after it when I can poke check it. I like that style and it works for me. Robb is good at figuring out each goalie's strengths and weaknesses and then he kind of custom-makes a program or style for each of them. It's cool, I love it." — **Joe Dawson, Plays at Hill Murray High School**

****

"Brent enjoys his time at the Goalcrease immeasurably. Personally, I don't know a lot about goaltending, but my son loves it and we wanted to get him the best possible instruction that we could. That is why we go to the Goalcrease, they are just outstanding at what they do. The facility is just marvelous. Their amenities are first class for the kids and there is a very comfortable viewing area for the parents too. They put the kids through a really intense work-out and training regimen and then they give them a lot of feedback afterwards. Then they work on all of the things that they need to work on and go through the entire process over and over until the kids master certain skills. They are outstanding coaches there and they really have the respect and attention of the kids. They customize each kids' practice to his or her own level and that is nice to see. They don't talk down to the kids either, they take it very seriously there and that is why they are so successful. Beyond that, it is nice to see them mold and shape your kids in a way that you as parents can't do." — **John Hollerud, Son Brent Plays Bantams in Blaine**

"I have been going to his camps for six years now and I love going there. Our entire youth hockey association uses the Goalcrease now too and that has been great for everybody. If I ever feel like I am having a rough time after a bad game or something, I always look forward to going in to see Robb. I know that they will get me straightened out and fix whatever isn't working right. I have gotten a lot better every time I have gone there and it has really made me a better goalie. It works 100% that is for sure. Robb is pretty friendly but he is also pretty serious when we are out on the ice. He will tell it to you like it is and sometimes that might not be what you want to hear. We do so many cool drills that you can totally use in games. He works a lot on the basic fundamentals too, like your footwork and your foundation. The Staubar helped me keep my arms where they are supposed to be and that worked really well too. He teaches us how to train and what we can be doing in practices in order to keep getting better. He knows so much and it is great to learn stuff from somebody who has so much experience and who played in the NHL. I have just steadily gotten better and better thanks to the Goalcrease. My saves percentage was above .900 this year and my goals-against was under 3.0. Plus I went from one shut-out last year to five this year, so those are pretty good numbers. My confidence is way up too and that is probably the most important thing of all." — **Brent Hollerud, Plays Bantams in Blaine**

****

"Our overall experience at the Goalcrease has been exceptional. All of the instructors there are very good and each one brings something a little different to the table. Robb does a great job of working with the goalies on both the technical side as well as on the mental side. He is an excellent teacher. He tells the kids right away what he expects from them and the reasons why they are going to be learning the things he will teach them. He explains each technique very thoroughly and then works with each kid until they get it. He watches them closely and then corrects them if they are doing something incorrectly. I can tell right away when Mike takes time off from seeing Robb. He isn't as mentally sharp, he is less sure of himself and he lets in more soft goals. It all comes back to confidence. So, it definitely makes a difference when he sees him regularly or not. Most of his coaches in Osseo don't know a lot about goaltending, so this is a win-win for everybody. Robb works with his coaches too, so that they are all on the same page with regards to what he is being taught. Overall, it is absolutely worth the investment." — **Jerry Taffe, Son Mike Plays Bantams in Osseo**

"My time at the Goalcrease has been very enjoyable and it has helped me a lot. Knowing that I am improving every time I go there is one of my biggest motivating factors. Robb always helps me whenever I need it and that is pretty cool. All of the instructors are great and it is just fun to go work-out there. They teach you the fundamentals in a way that is fun yet challenging. They helped me become faster and quicker on my feet. They also helped me with my angles and with my confidence. I just can't say enough good stuff about it, I highly recommend it to anyone who wants to be a better goalie. I have been to other camps and nothing comes close to this. At most of the other camps you are just a target out there, but the Goalcrease really teaches you on a one-on-one basis that is fun." — **Mike Taffe, Plays Bantams in Osseo**

****

"Robb runs our goalie camps for us and we couldn't be more pleased. He comes in to our rink to work with the kids once a week and that has been just wonderful for us. Working with Robb means you are working with the best, so our kids are very fortunate. He is a great teacher to the kids and brings so much knowledge of the game with him. He breaks down the skills for the kids and makes it really easy for them to understand. Robb gets the kids to really focus on what they are trying to achieve. He breaks down the mental as well as the physical with the kids and that is so important. He really emphasizes movement and footwork with our kids too, which is great. He teaches them about angles, about using proper edges and about being able to move in straight lines. It is a comprehensive curriculum that he teaches, and all of it is done according to the appropriate skill levels of the kids he is working with. We have seen a big improvement with our kids and much of that can be attributable to Robb and his staff.

"The repetition and the personal attention are all great, as is the Staubar, which has also helped significantly. Our program is turning out some really good goalies now and we also won our first state tournament title in more than 50 years, so things are definitely pointing in the right direction with our program. Some of the credit for that goes to Robb. It is truly a great opportunity for our kids to be able to work with somebody like that. His entire staff is great and they all have their own unique things to add to the mix." — **Carl Davis, Longtime Wayzata Boys High School Hockey Coach**

****

"Jon decided to play a couple years of junior hockey before going on to play Division One hockey. He had a lot of success working with Robb and that helped him a lot. Most goalie schools pile as many kids as possible in there in order to lower their costs. Well, the Goalcrease doesn't do that. They give the kids so much one-on-one time there and that is so important. What is so unique about Robb is the fact that there are just not that many good goaltenders who are good coaches. So, that really sets him apart. Goalie coaches are pretty hard to come by. In fact, I don't think there is one dedicated full-time goalie coach in the entire USHL, which is regarded by many as the premier junior hockey league in America. The Goalcrease is a place goalies like my son can go to nowadays just to get tune-ups and work on very specific things. That is what sets them apart from the others too, they can work with elite older college kids as well as peewees just starting out. Robb is extremely dedicated to his goaltenders and he is a very good teacher. He always makes the time to spend with the kids and really goes above and beyond in order to make them the best they can be. The bottom line is that Robb works very, very hard and runs a first class organization. I have a lot of respect for him." — **Lanny Anderson, Son Jon Played at White Bear Lake High School & Later Junior A Hockey in Montana; Will Eventually Play Division One**

"I have known Paul Ostby since I was a little kid and he is great. When I started coming to Goalcrease I got to know Robb too, and he is a great guy as well. Both are super teachers and they have taught me a lot. When I go to the Goalcrease I get to work on so many areas of my game that I never get to in a normal practice with my team. There, we just take shots and work out, that's it. With Robb and Paul we break down specific stuff and really work on it until it sticks. They will tell me things such as if they were playing against me they would know exactly where to shoot to score on me. That is very cool. They can study you and break down your weaknesses like nobody I have ever known. These guys are so knowledgeable and know so much about the position and it is just great to work with them. They both played at a high level too so they have a lot of credibility. I mean when they say something or tell you to try something a new way, you do it because you just know that they know what they are talking about. The facility is great, the videotape is great, everything about the whole deal is just great. I really liked using the Staubar too, that really helped me. All of those little things just add up until you have so much confidence and that is what it is all about.

"For me, I used to flop around a lot when I was in high school. I got by because I am a pretty good athlete and I did whatever I could to just keep the puck out of the net. Then, when I started working with Robb, he taught me how to be efficient and not get so spread out. I usually just butterfly now and work hard on always being in position with the right angles in order to make saves. Being acrobatic might look cool, but it is very inefficient and wastes energy. Now, I save my athletic ability until I really need it for a big save. I try to make things as easy as I can for myself out there. It is all about footwork and positioning with them and once it clicks, it totally makes sense. That was huge for me. Another thing we work on a lot is 'putting pucks in the corner,' or practicing where to kick saves so that they can be cleared out of the crease. So, they are just great at working on specific things with you and then doing them over and over until you master them.

"Out of high school I tried out for several USHL teams but none of them signed me. They told me I was out of position too often and too acrobatic, which basically meant I was flopping around too much. Well, I worked with Robb on that and now those same coaches who turned me down a year ago are pretty much drooling over me. It was just incredible and I never would have had that without the Goalcrease. Now, I am looking at playing Division One college hockey and my future looks brighter than ever." — **Jon Anderson, Played at White Bear Lake High School & Later Junior A Hockey in Montana; Will Eventually Play Division One**

****

"Goaltending is changing, and it's the Goalcrease that changed it. After my first training session I was amazed at how detailed my movements must become. Even at the college level, I have never experienced such knowledgeable instruction and insight into the game of hockey." — **Ellen Brinkman, Senior Goaltender at St. Cloud State University**

****

"What I get here in 40 minutes on the ice, is like two full varsity practices. Being able to watch what I am doing here on the ice really helps me fix the small problems in my game." — **Alex Stalock, Recently Drafted by the NHL's San Jose Sharks**

****

"I enjoy training at the Goalcrease. After every session I leave knowing that I have improved my game. The instructors videotape every session so that you can visualize your improvements and the areas you need to improve on. All the instructors are there to make you the best goalie you can possibly be." — **Ali Boe, Sophomore Goaltender at Harvard University**

DON LUCIA, HEAD COACH AT THE UNIVERSITY OF MINNESOTA

"As our goalie coach Robb has done a terrific job for us. He has really worked hard to develop our goaltenders and to teach them things that we couldn't do. Most importantly, he was able to get Adam Hauser and Travis Webber to play the best hockey of their careers in the NCAA playoffs, when it mattered most. So, Robb's influence certainly played a role in our program's back-to-back National Championships in 2002 & 2003. Robb has a quiet demeanor and is very patient. The kids respect him because he has been there and because he is a really good person. He enjoys the teaching aspect of coaching too, which is why he is so good at it.

Don Lucia

"To have Robb with us at the University of Minnesota is just wonderful. A lot of teams don't have goalie coaches so we are very fortunate in that regard. I mean our sport as a whole is finally getting out of the dark ages when it comes to that. Look at football, they have quarterback coaches and kicker coaches, but in hockey up until very recently having a goalie coach was unheard of. It is such a unique, specialized position too that unless you have played it and truly understand the mental and physical nuances of it, then you really can't coach it properly. You can argue that the goaltender is the quarterback of your team, your most valuable player — yet many teams don't give him the training that he really needs to thrive. So, Robb is really invaluable to our staff. To have somebody with that kind of experience and expertise is so reassuring. With Robb I can focus on coaching the other guys and let him handle the goaltenders, that frees me a up to do what I do best.

"It is wonderful to see Robb's success with the Goalcrease. When you go there and see the whole setup it is so impressive. It is such a unique training facility and there is really nothing else like it. I would say that it is a first of its kind and in that regard he is a pioneer in many ways. He has created a top notch facility there, perfect for training goaltenders. And that is something that has sorely been needed in the profession. I think it is going to pay big dividends for him as more and more kids go there and then reap the rewards of his outstanding teaching and coaching. Robb is just a quality person and I wish him nothing but the best."

DOUG WOOG, FORMER HEAD COACH AT THE UNIVERSITY OF MINNESOTA

"Robbie is just a first class guy and I am really proud of him. He is one of my all-time favorites and I couldn't be happier for his success. On the ice, it was always an adventure with him out there. He kept us on our toes, that was for sure. He made the most of his opportunity with us at Minnesota though and really appreciated the entire experience. He was proud to be a Gopher and to wear the Maroon and Gold. Those are the types of people that you look back at and feel really good about. He went on to have a good career in the NHL for a number of years too, which was fantastic. Now he is making the most of his life by giving back to young people and that is just great to see.

Doug Woog

"Robbie always did things his own way and that is still true of him today. He loved to come out and play the puck, something goaltenders are not usually known for, but that was his style. He was very unconventional and really changed the landscape for future goaltenders with regards to how they could handle the puck. The guy was fearless out there and liked to challenge guys. He loved to start a break-out and thought of himself as a sixth forward when they were on offense. The way he played was revolutionary in a lot of ways. He really changed the way goalies are viewed and that is one of the reasons he was the first goaltender ever to win the Hobey Baker Award. He just was very unorthodox and wanted to do things his own way. As a coach it was good and bad. He drove me nuts on more than one occasion when he would came out to the blue line to challenge a skater, but he usually came out on top. He was an independent, free-spirit kind of a guy and he was a fierce competitor too. He was so good, such a great player. We were lucky to have him, he was such an asset to our program. Yeah, they broke the mold on

Robbie, he was truly a one-of-a-kind.

"So, to see him now having success at the Goalcrease is really nice. I run a hockey camp now and we love it when our goalies take lessons with him. He is the best at what he does and he is a great teacher. He has a passion for what he does and he wants to pass that along to these kids. He is a pretty down-to-earth kind of guy and he can explain things to kids in a way that they can understand. Robbie is just a smart guy and is having great success doing something that he loves to do. That is the definition of happiness in my book. I wish him nothing but the best."

BARRY MELROSE, FORMER NHL HEAD COACH & CURRENT ESPN HOCKEY ANALYST

"I remember the first time I saw Robb playing in an American Hockey League game, he was just unbelievable. I could see early on that he was going to be something special. When you looked at him out there he just grabbed your attention really quickly. I coached his brother Pete at that time and asked him a lot of questions about him. Robb's team wasn't that good but he kept his guys in it and gave them a chance to win — which is a sign of a great goaltender. Physically, Robb was one of the most gifted goaltenders I have ever seen. His athletic ability was just off the chart. He could do so many things that a lot of other goalies couldn't dream of; things like shooting the puck; stick handling the puck; and his mobility and vision on the ice were just

Barry Melrose

incredible. He was just an immense physical talent and I had a lot of respect for him in that regard.

"When I came to the L.A. Kings in 1993 I made the move to bring him back up from the minors. We brought him up to be our No. 2 goalie behind Kelly Hrudy. We were going to ease him in and just let him learn under Kelly, who had been a solid NHL goaltender for several years by then. The two of them rotated and it worked out well for us. At one point Robb won like 11 straight games for us and was really on a roll. He was just so exciting to watch too, the fans loved him. His glove was so quick and he could skate all over the place, which was always an adventure with him. He loved to stickhandle and the fans loved to see him come out of his crease to do his thing. As a coaching staff we weren't thrilled about that, but as long as he was winning we weren't going to say too much. All in all, he was just a pleasure to watch out there.

"I remember in the 1993 playoffs when he got on a nice roll against Calgary and Vancouver en route to us making it all the way to the Stanley Cup Finals against Montreal. Kelly had struggled early on and Robb came in to be the hero. It was a pretty amazing story for this young kid to have so much success that early in his career. Against Calgary, specifically, Robb played so well. I mean they had a great team with guys like Al McGinnis, Gary Sutter, Theo Fleurry, Joe Nieuwendyk and Mike Vernon in goal. They were an outstanding hockey club and we beat them pretty good thanks to Robb's three victories for us.

"I can recall at least a half dozen times that year when a player would come in on break-away and the second he would put his head down to look at the puck, Robb would come screaming out of his crease and slide right into him. It was unbelievable. Usually the player was so shocked to see the goalie come that far out to challenge him that he would freeze for a split second to try and comprehend what was going on. Well, by then Robbie was plowing into his legs, sending him ass over tea kettle down the ice. Man, the fans used to just love that stuff, they would go wild.

"That 1993 season was just magical. Aside from our Cup run it seemed like everything went right for us. One of my favorite stories about Robb from that year which I will never forget was when his wife won a bunch of money on the TV show "The Price is Right," with Bob Barker. A bunch of the hockey wives went on the show one time and sure enough, she was chosen to be a contestant. She didn't disappoint either, she won big and we all got a big kick out of that. We even tried to tease him about it and how he could be expecting a smaller contract the next time around because he had so much dough coming in. That was hilarious!

"Robb was a quiet leader and definitely not one of the loudest guys in the locker-room. He was just the polar opposite of Kelly Hrudy, who was loud, aggressive and extremely extroverted. Robb tried to lead by example, just sitting back and listening a lot. And hey, with guys like Wayne Gretzky on your team it was pretty easy to just let it all soak in. He was a really hard working guy though and very professional. As a coach my philosophy was that if you out-work your opponents you will beat them 90% of the time, no matter what. Robb had a great work ethic and it showed in practice. He was always prepared to play and always had a positive attitude out on the ice. He never complained either, he just kept his mouth shut and waited for his turn to get into the game. As a coach you loved working with guys like Robb Stauber. He was very smart and concentrated a great deal on making good decisions out on the ice. His teammates definitely respected him and that says a lot.

"Who knows how good Robbie could have been had it not been for all of his injuries. That was too bad but sometimes that is just hockey. He never really got the opportunity to become the goaltender he could have become because of that, which was unfortunate. I mean had it not been for his injuries he would probably still be playing in the NHL. He was that good. He was just an immense talent. It was too bad because it seemed like every time he got on a good roll something bad would happen to him. I know that frustrated him to no end. And believe me, it was just as frustrating for me as the coach because I could never count on him for a full season. Having your goaltender play well consistently adds a lot to your team's chemistry and when Robb was out all the time it disrupted everything.

"As a person Robb is a smart guy and you could tell that he was very well educated and very well spoken. There are a lot of guys in our line of work who didn't go to school, as well as a lot of others who did go — but just as a stepping stone to get into the league. Robb wasn't like that. You could tell that he had his head screwed on straight and that he had plans for himself after hockey. I think that is why he sat back so much and watched and listened the way he did. He was soaking it all in and learning as much as he could. He was a very good listener and genuinely wanted to learn more and more so that he could get better. That was refreshing to see as a coach. He had a real passion for the game and was just one of those guys who was always thinking about it — day and night.

"As a testimonial for Robb's Goalcrease, I can say very proudly that I would not hesitate for a second to send my kids there. Robb is a great person and I know that his heart is in the right place. As a teacher I am sure that Robb gets his students extremely well prepared because that was the way he played the game night in and night out. I know that he runs his academy very professionally and that he is on top of every little detail. That is the way he is and in hockey that is a tremendous quality. I know that his kids will be well coached, well supervised and that they will definitely learn a great deal about how to play the game the right way. They will learn to play the position with pride and with respect too, I can guarantee you that."

MARTY McSORLEY, FORMER L.A. TEAMMATE

"I first met Robb when he came to the L.A. Kings as a rookie. He was just oozing with raw talent. I spent some time with him in training camp and got to know him a little bit. We knew that he was a talented kid, having won the Hobey Baker Award, and were anxious to see his stuff at the NHL level. Robb was a quiet guy but definitely had strong opinions on things that mattered to him. When Robb joined our club it was a really fun time to be a King. We were just on the verge of going places and had a lot of new faces in camp that year. We could all sense the energy early on that year and it was just an exciting time for us.

"I remember a funny story

Marty McSorley

about Robb's first season in L.A. It was about January I think and I saw Robb in the training room getting some treatment for an injury. We talked for a while and he told me that he was living in a crappy apartment way out in Lonsdale and was commuting in for therapy. I couldn't believe he was driving that far everyday to come in just for treatment. Well, I went to the coaching staff later that day and told them the situation. I told them that here was this really talented rookie who was basically dying on the vine, being secluded because of his injury. Robb was too modest to hang out in the locker-room with the guys because he felt like he needed to earn their respect first out on the ice. So, he just laid low and tried to train as much as he could while he was recovering.

"Anyway, that next night we had a game and afterwards I saw Robb standing in the corner of the locker-room wearing a suit and tie, just looking awkward as ever. I went over to him and said 'How ya doing kid?' He says 'pretty good.' Then I asked him laughing 'The coaches told you to show up didn't they?' He just smiled and after a long pause said 'Ah... Yup!' I still laugh thinking about that. Robb was just such a modest guy and wanted to feel like he had earned his spot in there, I totally respected that about him. From then on he started hanging out with us more at both practices and at games, which was great. He wasn't totally comfortable with the fact that he wasn't playing and paying his dues, but he wanted to fit in. Robb was a stand-up guy and despite the fact that he didn't play much his first season, it didn't take long for his teammates to give him their respect.

"I remember another time skating out in front of Robb during a game and hearing him yell at the opposing player who had the puck to shoot it. He was screaming 'Shoot it!' - 'Shoot it!', daring the guy to challenge him. Robb was a serious competitor and he was just in the zone when he was out there. I swear he thought he was a winger out there too, I mean he just loved to handle the puck and pass it out. He also loved to come out and challenge guys as soon as he saw them come at him on a break-away. It was amazing to watch because you could see it happening from a mile away. Robb would slide right into him to poke check the puck away, usually knocking the guy right over the top of him. It was risky but very effective. Most goaltenders couldn't do that because they either weren't fast enough or didn't have the balls to do it. Well, Robb did.

"Robb was a just a good professional. To be a good professional means a lot of things. First, you have to be a fan of the game. That was Robb. He loved to talk hockey all the time and was really a fan first. He loved to watch games and he did a lot of research about the players, to study them and their tendencies. Beyond that, I think Robb was a perfectionist and was always striving to be the best he could possibly be. He was a very quiet guy, but he led by example in other ways. He always showed up to compete and guys respected him for that. He prided himself on being so tough in practice too, which as a player, you totally loved. That brought the work ethic of the entire team up to another level. Conversely, a bad goalie who doesn't try in practice, can just ruin a team's mental preparation in practice. So, he just wanted to challenge you no matter what and he hated to lose.

"Robb also dealt very well with the fact that he was a back-up most of the time. He understood his role and he prepared himself to start every game should they need him, and that was how he went about his business. Robb showed up prepared and ready to go night in and night out, no matter what. He was also very supportive of Kelly, his partner and the team's No. 1 goaltender. A lot of guys wouldn't do that, but Robb was all about the team and the guys knew that. Then, when his number finally did get called, he was all over it. I mean back in '93 when we made our Stanley Cup run, Robb won some huge games for us and carried us on his back at times. As players we knew that he was never going to cheat us out of his best effort on any given night and that meant a lot to us. He brought us up a notch, he really did.

"So, you take all of that, and then you can see why Robb is so good at working with kids. He is a true professional. Robb has been there and has so much credibility. Kids look up to him and respect him. He is a very hard worker too and also very intelligent. Plus, he is so modest. He just wants to do what is best for each individual kid and that is what it is all about. Now that I am a coach I really respect guys like Robb for how they go about their business. Young goaltenders should consider themselves really lucky to get a teacher as good as Robb Stauber. He understands goaltending as an art and is truly an artist."

MARTY McSORLEY ON GOALTENDING IN GENERAL...

"I think that goaltenders have to be careful not to put themselves into isolation. A lot of guys look at goalies and say 'Goalies are weird, just leave them alone to do their own thing...'. Some of them are weird, no question, but there is a difference between being odd and being a loner. Some of them are so focused on what they have to do that they don't want guys messing with them. A lot of them are really superstitious too. Many of them tend to focus a great deal on their practice preparation and on their equipment. As a result, the other guys oftentimes tend to just stay out of their way. I don't know if that is good or bad, it is just the reality of a lot of goaltenders I think. Everybody prepares for a game differently, but certainly goaltenders are in a league all by themselves in that matter.

"Things have come a long way though in how we treat and interact with goaltenders. I will never forget during my rookie year in the NHL every player was forbidden from speaking to the goaltender on the day of a game. How nuts was that? We didn't speak to them between periods either, they were just on an island all by themselves and apparently that was how they liked it. That has changed nowadays and that is certainly for the better. Some goalies weren't like that at all though, guys like Marty Brodeur. He wasn't too mental about anything and as a result he had a lot of fun and was able to play a lot of games. That mental pressure those guys put themselves under has to take a toll. It is a lot of stress to carry and I think eventually it catches up with them at some point. Most goalies are perfectionists and you simply can't be perfect at that position. It is impossible. Their game itself is much more individual than the rest of the team and coaches have to handle their goaltenders just a little bit differently from the other guys. They have to deal with them in a manner that will not hurt their confidence or mess them up. A lot of coaches won't admit to that, but it is the truth.

"I will also say that you're goaltender is your best player, period. Take any successful team and nine times out of ten the MVP of that team is the goalie. It has even become more so in recent years with the emphasis on defense. You can't have a great season without having great goaltending. The only time I ever saw that was when Detroit won the Cup with Chris Osgood, and that was some time ago. No player will ever score two or three goals per game, but a good goaltender will be worth two to three more saves per game than a second tier goaltender. They are difference makers and they can swing the momentum big-time for a team."

MIKE GREENLAY, FORMER NHL GOALIE & CURRENT MINNESOTA WILD TV ANALYST

ON ROBB & THE GOALCREASE...

"Robb is a terrific person, but then again so is his entire family. Robb's brother Pete was my roommate in college when we played at Lake Superior State together. So, I used to go back to Duluth in the Summers to stay with their family and they are all just wonderful people. They are like family to me. You can see where Robb gets his down to earth attitude after spending time with them, they are just hard working, decent people. As for Robb the coach, he is so talented. He works so hard with his kids and has completely earned the respect of the entire hockey community with what he is doing. He is really making a difference and that is great to see.

"As for the Goalcrease, it is absolutely state of the art, just amazing. This is serious business just for goalies and that is what makes it so unique. And do you know what the best part of it is? It is just for goalies! Ha!, just for us, nobody else and that is awesome. You never see anything just for goalies and that is so long overdue. When you go in there as a goalie you

Mike Greenlay

come out of there as a goalie. You are not coming out as a defenseman or something, which is what you see sometimes at other Summer camps and stuff. That is why the Goalcrease is so important, it is the first of its kind and really makes a big difference with those kids. It focuses on one thing and it does it better than anybody else, period.

"I think back to what my life would have been like had I been able to go to a place like that when I was a kid. I mean I knew more about goaltending than almost all of my youth coaches put together. It was so frustrating because none of the coaches could explain things to me very well. My parents sent me to a ton of camps when I was a kid up in Canada, but it was nothing like the Goalcrease. When you go to a Summer camp you just take shots while the coaches work with the forwards and defensemen all day. At the Goalcrease they work with those kids all day every day in a one-on-one setting which does nothing but build those kids' confidence. It is like anything else in life, such as school for instance. When you get one-on-one training and focused attention from really educated teachers or tutors who care about you, then you learn and improve must faster and much better."

ON THE STATE OF THE STATE OF
GOALTENDING AT THE YOUTH LEVELS...

"Goaltending has gone from being the fat kid who couldn't skate, a la the right fielder who was the last kid picked, to oftentimes being the best athlete on the team. That is my take on goaltending today, it has really changed — and that is just great to see. Now kids fight over who gets to play in goal. Everything about it has changed and become much 'cooler' for kids, starting with the equipment and the fancy masks — which all the kids want to wear. I think there has been a fundamental change or mental shift as to how goaltending is now perceived. Kids know that you can touch the puck and be a part of the action. You can be a difference maker in the game and beyond that it is fun. Sure, there is a lot of pressure with it and it is a very competitive position, but that is what makes it so exciting."

ON WHY SHOULD KIDS BE GOALIES
TODAY VERSUS OTHER POSITIONS...

"It depends on your competitive nature I think. If you are a competitive kid, then goaltending can be great for you because it gives you a chance to make a big difference in any one game. If you are a forward or a defenseman, you may never touch the puck throughout an entire game. But if you are a goaltender I guarantee you that you will make a difference. Now, it might be a positive difference or it might be a negative difference, but you will have a say in the outcome of the game for sure. So, if you are a competitor and want to have that type of pressure put on you, then this is a great position to play."

ON THE NHL'S NEW RULE CHANGES FOR GOALIES...

"Thank goodness they did not decide to make the net bigger, that would have been a disaster. I mean come on, at some point if you put a soccer net out there, sure, they are going to let some goals in and increase the scoring league-wide! Having said that, I think it was a good decision to reduce the size of the equipment by 11%, because it has gotten out of control. The leg pads are much wider, the pants or breezers have big flairs on the sides and the shoulder and chest protectors make 180 pound guys look like they are about 350. So, that is all good and it will open up the offense out there the way that they want to. I mean players used to score goals off of goalies' hips, under their arms, and off the sides of their legs, but you don't hardly see that anymore. You have goalies who are much more athletic than in years past wearing huge equipment and the result has been much fewer goals scored. It will take some getting used to, but in the long run I think this is really good for hockey."

DON BEAUPRE, FORMER GOALTENDER WITH THE MINNESOTA NORTH STARS

ON ROBB & THE GOALCREASE...

"I first met Robb when he was playing at the U of M. I remember being very impressed with him and knowing that he had what it took to make it in the NHL. We eventually played against each other in the minor leagues when he was on his way up and I was on my way down. He was a great player and someone who I felt was very professional about the way he went about his business. I coach my kids a little bit these days so I have a great respect for what Robb does as a teacher. His academy is a great thing and I am happy for all of his success. It is great for young goaltenders to have a place like that to go to learn the game the right way."

Don Beaupre

ON WHAT IT TAKES TO SUCCEED AS A GOALTENDER...

"The bottom line for me is hard work. The higher the level you go in hockey, the harder you have to work. You have to put in the time in practice to train and you have to study the position to get better. Don't shortchange yourself or your teammates by not working your hardest in practice. That is where you learn confidence and that is where you earn respect from your teammates. You also have to work on being focused and on improving your mental side of the game. Confidence is something you build on and gain slowly, but once you have it, that is when you will really start to see results. Beyond that some of the best advice I can give young goaltenders is to simply watch a lot of hockey games. Go to the games if you can and watch warm-ups, otherwise watch them on TV. Study what they are doing and really watch and learn what is happening out there. If you do, you just might learn something too. Beyond that, I think the biggest thing for young kids today who want to be goaltenders is for them to work on the fundamentals. That has to be the most important thing, otherwise they will never make it at the higher levels."

ON BEING THE BACK-UP...

"One bit of advice I would have for goaltenders who are not the clear-cut No. 1 on their squad is for them to have patience. When I was with the North Stars for all those years I had to wait and pay my dues behind Gilles Meloche. Sure, it was tough at times, but I understood my role as the No. 2. I looked at Gilles as a mentor and just tried to learn as much as I could from him. We had different styles but I certainly looked up to him, especially early on in my career. Gilles was older than me and that helped our dynamic together, which was nice. I mean we were roommates on the road and spent all of our time together in practices, so if we didn't get along that would have been really tough. I know the competition can be frustrating, but you just have to make the most of your opportunities whenever they present themselves. Whether that means playing great in the last minutes of a game that is a blow-out or being prepared to start a game that you weren't expecting to — you have to be ready. You need to be prepared even during the games you aren't starting because you never know if the other guy might get injured early in a game and you have to jump in cold. So, stay positive, encourage your partner, and be ready — your time will come if you work hard in practice and show the coaches that you are a team player. Plus, your teammates will respect you for that and they will be on your side when it does come time for you to get in there."

ON DEALING WITH A TOUGH LOSS...

"Losses are never fun. They are always easier if you played your best though. I just tried to stay focused and positive if I had a really bad one. You just have to pick yourself up pretty quickly and get ready for your next game. I always tried to learn from my mistakes and then move on. You can never let yourself get too high or too low as a goaltender, that is just the nature of the position. It is tough to be the goalie and to let up a soft goal in overtime or something. The fans boo you and you feel terrible. You feel like you let your teammates down and it is tough, but you just have to take it game by game and try harder the next time. When you let in a goal the fans immediately think it was your fault, they don't understand many times that there was a defensive breakdown or that somebody messed up down the ice way before the goal was scored. Maybe it was on a power play because of a dumb penalty. There are so many things that go into a goal being scored other than just the shot itself. So, you just have to stay positive and not let yourself dwell on things for too long or you will lose your confidence. As a goalie you're only as good as your last game but certainly winning cures all. Nothing is better for your confidence than a big win."

ADVICE FOR PARENTS...

"Goaltending is such an under coached position and that is tough. So, I think parents should be involved to help their kids when they can. If that means helping out the coaches or working overtime to get their kid the attention he or she needs on the ice, so be it. Certainly, if you have the means to get your son or daughter some extra instruction, like at Robb's academy, then that would be the best scenario. To have your kid get instruction from any trained professional is a great thing and something I wish more kids could take advantage of.

"Parents also need to recognize early on whether or not their kid really sincerely enjoys stopping pucks or if they just like the cool equipment. There is a big difference there and finding that out early on is the key. Chances are they are not going to last in goal if they truly don't love being in there. It just clicks for some kids, they love being in there and it fits. For others you have to realize that maybe it just wasn't meant to be, and that can be tough. As parents though, you have to give your kids the best opportunity that you can in order for them to see if they can succeed at the position. Kids need a lot of instruction early on to get down the fundamentals, otherwise they just aren't going to get it. And, if they do get it, oftentimes they pick up a lot of bad habits that will have to be broken later on, which can be very difficult. So, you have to applaud the parents who do take the time to go out of their way to try to find their kids good instruction and help them that way."

BOB MASON, FORMER NHL GOALIE & CURRENT MINNESOTA WILD GOALIE COACH

ON THE STATE OF THE STATE OF GOALTENDING TODAY...

"I think it is great to tell you the truth. We are seeing bigger, more athletic kids wanting to be goalies, whereas before it used to be 'put the kid who can't skate back in the net...'. Well, those days are over. Now, you have the skill guys getting in the net and that has really changed the game in a lot of ways. In many ways goaltending has become a glamour position and that has certainly attracted more top level kids to the position."

Bob Mason

ADVICE FOR YOUNG GOALIES...

"I would say play a lot and don't worry so much about winning and losing. Try to develop your footwork skills and work on the fundamentals, that is so important. I would also say don't emulate guys who play on their knees. It is OK to emulate NHL goalies, but don't ever get too comfortable going down to your knees too much. Develop your foot skills and be good on your feet. You will go much further in this game if you can do that. As you get older, maybe into bantams and midgets, you will develop your own style. Don't get too focused on any one thing, just have an open mind and try to do a lot of different things. The most important thing though, is footwork. Beyond that, always try to make progress talent-wise and just keep working on improving your game. Work out in the Summer and train hard to stay in shape. Progression is the key to getting better. Once you start flat-lining, it gets pretty tough to get any better and that is when guys fall off pretty quickly."

ON JOB-SHARING...

"I would say to guys to just hang in there and pay your dues. I mean I played on the junior varsity as a junior in high school but still went on to become an NHL goaltender. So, it can happen. I had to wait until my senior year before I was 'The Guy' and that was tough. But, I made the best of it by learning from the guys ahead of me and supporting them whenever I could. I put the team first and my teammates really respected that I think. Beyond that, I think that friendly competition is healthy. I mean I was always very competitive with my partner wherever I played, whether that was up in my home town of International Falls or with the Chicago Blackhawks. I wanted to be better than him, so I tried to work harder than he did in practice. No matter what, if you play hard in practice and give it your all, your coaches will take notice and eventually good things will happen to you. Sooner or later you will close that gap and your opportunity will present itself. If you are going to get a 'label' make sure it is for being a 'worker,' because coaches love workers.

"Beyond that, always battle and never give up. That is so important. Sometimes it can be tough. I mean you are typically roommates with your goalie partner on the road and you become pretty good friends with each other. So, you have to be supportive as well as be able to push one another so that you both get better. It is a fine line and that can be difficult, no question. I deal with Manny Fernandez and Duane Roloson now with the Wild and those guys really work well together. They are very supportive and encourage each other to play their best. Sure, they battle in practice and are extremely competitive with each other, but they understand that the coaches will ultimately decide which of them will play on any given night. That type of positive attitude and cooperation really helps the entire team chemistry. I think the competition also forces them to stay sharp mentally, which is good too. You know, I don't know of any goalie who wants to rotate and have a partner, they all want to be 'The Guy,' no matter what. But, that is not realistic all the time, so they have to make the best of whatever situation that they are in."

WARREN STRELOW, LONGTIME NHL GOALIE COACH, CURRENTLY WITH THE SAN JOSE SHARKS

ON THE STATE OF THE STATE OF GOALTENDING TODAY...

"I think that it is in good shape. A lot more kids are interested in the position and the quality of those kids has improved greatly over the years. It used to be the kid who couldn't skate very well was always thrown back in goal, well not any more. Kids who want to be goaltenders now are some of the best athletes on the team. That has changed things a lot for the better."

Warren Strelow

ADVICE FOR YOUNG GOALIES...

"Aside from working on the fundamentals, I would say that you have to be quick on your feet. Movement is the key to success at this position and without it you are going to fail. I have been an NHL goalie coach for two decades now and still preach movement every single day. That has not changed since I have been around and I don't think it will change any time in the future either. If you can't move around in net, then you aren't going to have a chance to stop the puck. Lateral movement, balance and agility, that is where it all starts. If you are diving around for shots on the ice, you are way out of position. So, you need to start there. Then, you need to learn your angles, that is really important too. I am not a fan of goalies who go down all the time either. You have to stay on your feet and then read and react, that is the key. Let the game come to you. If you work on those things you will have success at whatever level you are playing at, guaranteed. Remember, be patient, read the oncoming rush, analyze it quickly and then be confident in your ability to make the right move for that particular situation. Keep your composure and you will be fine."

ADVICE FOR PARENTS...

"I would tell them to try to be understanding. Don't put a lot of pressure on your kids, especially if they are young. They have to like to play the position in order to have success at it, that is important. If you are constantly on them every time they make a mistake and make them feel bad then they are going to lose their confidence. Look, there are two parts to goaltending: the physical part, which are the fundamentals; and the mental part, which deals with handling adversity, pressure and stress. The mental part is much tougher to fix than the physical, don't forget that. Good goalies learn how to rebound after a poor performance and remain focused. They also stay on an even keel when they win so that they don't get too high afterwards and lose their focus for the next game. So, help them with those things and you will be doing them a great service. Most importantly they will have fun, and that is the key."

ADVICE FOR COACHES...

"Work with your kids but don't try to change them. You can help to perfect their weaknesses but you don't want to change their style. Just work with what style that they are comfortable with and focus on helping them to get better from within that framework. If they like to stand up versus butterfly, then work with that and build their confidence from there. I think the best scenario is a combination of the two, a hybrid, which is the best of both worlds in my opinion. Perfect their weaknesses and try to improve their skill level by practicing and working hard. Work on their mental toughness, it is so important that they stay strong and focused out there. Then, really work with them on not letting in bad goals. There are good goals and bad goals, and bad goals will kill you. If they stop all of the easy ones and three quarters of the tough ones, then they will be just fine — remember that.

"Another really big thing is to never yell at or brow-beat your goalie in front of the guys. Never. That will crush their confidence and then you are back to square one with them. If he has a bad goal or a bad game, you just focus on rebounding from that and get that bad game out of their mind. Sure, work on the bad parts of that game at the next practice, but then move on and concentrate on your next opponent. It is like an NFL kicker sometimes, they don't lose their ability to kick field goals, they just lose their confidence. You need to be smart on how you build them back up after they get down and that is all about trust and communication.

"I would also say that if a goaltender goes into a slump, and they all do from time to time, they need to find their way out as quickly as possible. You try to avoid slumps, but they are inevitable from time to time I think. To avoid them you need to consistently work on your fundamentals and do drills that reinforce those things. Keep working and eventually you will get through it, just stay strong mentally, that is the key. Again, never yell or criticize your goalie in the locker-room where other guys can see you or hear you because that is just going to hurt their confidence. Talk to them calmly and work with them in private. You need to create a bond so that they will trust you. Many of my goaltenders have told me that they view me as their second father and I take that as a great honor. So, confidence and trust are just as important as ability.

"I am also not a big fan of pulling goalies when they are not doing well. I remember when I was coaching out with the New Jersey Devils with Herb Brooks, I think I pulled my guy once that entire season. Once! It can be a real stigma for those guys to have to come off the ice in the middle of a period. It can be an effective wake up call, however, not only for the goalie but for the entire team if used properly. But, be careful of that and only use it as a last resort when they are really struggling. Don't let them take all the blame either, especially if the defense wasn't doing their job properly. Tell your goalies when they do well and let them know when you are proud of them, they need to hear that. And remember, they know darn well if they did-n't play well in a tough loss — you don't need to remind them of that either."

PAUL OSTBY, FORMER PROFESSIONAL GOALTENDER & CURRENT DIRECTOR OF TRAINING AT THE GOALCREASE

ON ROBB...

"I first met Robb back in the mid-1980s when he was a freshman at the University of Minnesota. I was his goalie coach with the Gophers and we hit it off right away. Robb wound up having such an amazing career there and it was a lot of fun working with him. Every day was a new challenge for me as a coach with Robb. He was one of those rare athletes who doesn't come around very often. He forced me as a coach to constantly get better just to keep up with him. He was just that good. As a player, Robb was a bulldog. He was so tough and relentless. He was such an intense competitor, yet he had a calmness about him that separated him from the other guys.

Paul Ostby

"As for the genesis of the Goalcrease, Robb and I had been doing 'Stauber-Ostby' Summer goalie camps for about 10 years together after he left the University and he had always talked about the concept of doing a year-round academy. We added some Fall warm-up camps and then a Winter tune-up, followed by a Spring camp. Eventually we knew that their was a marketplace for a year-round camp or academy, but we didn't know how we were going to be able to pull it off. Robb took the ball and ran with it though and said he was going to make it happen no matter what. That was Robb, just so passionate and driven. I remember looking at him and thinking he was nuts. I mean how was he going to afford building a facility with its own ice? I was skeptical at first, but Robb was determined and sure enough he got it done. It is amazing what he has accomplished here and I am just proud to be a small part of it. This place has evolved into one of the premier training facilities in the world and we are all really proud of that

"Being able to work with him on a daily basis at the Goalcrease, I can see many of those same similarities between Robb the player and Robb the coach/businessman. He is just very goal oriented and has really high expectations for not only his clients, or kids, but also his staff. He works very hard and is very driven by success. He is very demanding on those who work with him, yet he takes extremely good care of them as well. Ultimately he is as hard on himself as he is anybody else. There is a lot of dialogue and feedback between Robb and the instructors on a daily and weekly basis, because he wants to make sure that they are always on the same page. He has an extremely deep sense of loyalty too, and is very passionate about what he does.

"So, Robb and I have worked together and been friends now for about 20 years and our relationship continues to grow and evolve every day. It has been really fun to work together but we have definitely had our challenges and disagreements along the way. We are always able to find common ground though and that is why we have had success together. We have some similarities as well as some deep contrasts in our coaching beliefs but we both want what is ultimately the best for our kids. Coming together for the benefit of our clients is what it is all about and that is why I think we have had so much success together. We are just able to communicate and that has been the glue which has held our friendship together for all these years. We have had our differences on many different things, absolutely, but we have always had a mutual respect for each other.

"Robb just has a vision and I am so grateful that he went out on a limb and made it happen. A lot of people talk a big game but Robb just very quietly goes out and does it. People really respect him for that. He is just an honest, hard working guy who loves working with kids. It is a great story. He is an entrepreneur, a risk taker and a dreamer — and those are all factors as to why he is so successful. His passion, dedication and focus is contagious, and that is why his staff enjoys working with him so much."

ON THE GOALCREASE...

"You know, the staff at the Goalcrease is just second to none. They are the backbone of the operation and their teaching and instruction is what makes it so great. It is a very diverse group of goalie coaches who each has their own area of expertise. I mean take a guy like Steve DeBus, who played at high school, in juniors, at the U of M, and even played some pro hockey. He has a ton of great experience as a player and he knows how to relate that experience to kids in a way that they can comprehend. Everybody there is unique but the common denominator with all of the coaches and instructors is their passion and dedication to teaching young people.

"Parents should know that if they send their kids to the Goalcrease that they will get an unparalleled commitment from the coaches. The one-on-one consultation is second to none there. The message is pretty much the same from all of them, which gives the kids a unique blend of diversity as well as consistency. It is very process oriented there too, where they reinforce the fundamentals on a daily, weekly and monthly basis. The videotaping in that regard is so valuable to the kids. For them to see what they are doing on a TV while sitting next to their instructor, who can explain what is going on, is such a powerful tool. It is all about the discipline, repetition and instruction on constantly improving to master skills. All of that builds confidence, which is the key to goaltending.

"Another huge bonus of coming to the Goalcrease is the whole issue of equipment. When kids buy new goalie equipment with us they have the option to be able to try it out and use it to see whether or not it works for them. Demo equipment is a totally new concept in retailing, but that is another thing kids can do with us. That is very significant because equipment is so expensive and takes time to break in properly. All of the coaches at the Goalcrease know how to properly size and fit kids too, so they work with them on selecting the right stuff. They will recommend things to them that pro shops wouldn't dream of, because most pro shop owners aren't professional goalie instructors. The staff just knows the kids and they know their tendencies out on the ice, which helps in properly fitting them. Having the right equipment is a big part of being comfortable and confident in goal.

"Sure, our facility is state of the art and probably the best in the business, but the neatest aspect of the Goalcrease is still the human element. The coaches really try to get to know these kids and help them to reach their full potential both on and off the ice. Kids get a variety of coaches and many different sets of eyes evaluating and working with them here. That is so important. So many goalie 'gurus' out there just have a 'my way or the highway' attitude, and that creates false dependencies between the athlete and the coach. Our philosophy is to work with kids on the fundamentals and on the psychological aspects of the game to the best of their abilities. We want to prepare these kids so that when they go out to play in a game, they will be independent of their coach and can think for themselves. We want them to internalize what they have learned and become reflexive, or reactive, without doing a lot of thinking. Then it just becomes second nature to make a certain move or to be in a certain position or to face a shooter from that angle when that particular scenario presents itself. All of those things will eventually become second nature and the position will become much easier to play. When that happens, success usually follows. That is when it is fun for us and really fun for the kids.

"You know, anytime you can work with kids and coach them to be better people, then that is wonderful. We get the opportunity to make an impact on young people's lives at the Goalcrease and that is very rewarding. Not only do we get to work with kids, but also their parents, which can be a very powerful tool in teaching. That reinforces training habits at home and makes sure that we are all on the same page. Helping people to get better is what it is all about. You can't reach every kid and not every kid can evolve into a great goaltender, or even a good goaltender for that matter. But that is the risk you take as a coach, to try your best with each kid and give it your best effort to help him or her reach their full potential. As a coach you are always open and susceptible to critics, and frankly I think that is good. You need to be accountable for your actions, that is what makes you better as a person and as a coach. If you learn from your mistakes and make changes, then you are growing and becoming stronger. My goal is to be the best coach

I can be so I want to do whatever it takes to achieve that.

"Dedication, passion and organization are what we are all about. Our concept on teaching is really different from the other camps that are out there. Are we more expensive than them? Yes, but we think we are worth it. And most importantly, our clients think we are worth it because they keep coming back and referring others to us. You know, if goaltending is your child's passion, then as parents I say encourage it and give them the best shot that you can to be successful. Believe me, you could spend your money on much worse things like wave runners, motorcycles, video games or what have you. Top notch instruction into one of the most specialized and unique sports positions that exists is a wonderful investment. Who knows where that investment will lead to? From what we have seen so far, it will lead to more confident kids who have better success and more fun. Those are pretty good dividends in my opinion. Beyond that, people have to realize that at the Goalcrease this is all these people do. They coach and instruct full-time year round, not just at Summer camps. I mean Robb does this 24/7 and has no other job. This is his dream, his career and his passion. He is committed 100% to his clients and to his kids, and it shows. I am just thrilled to be a part of it, I think we are really making a difference."

LAURA GIESELMAN-EVANSON, FORMER ST. COULD STATE GOALIE & CURRENT GOALCREASE INSTRUCTOR

ON THE GOALCREASE...

"It is such an exciting place to work, I really enjoy it. I love to see all of the kids come in every week and to watch their development. We have been a part of a lot of youth hockey associations over the past two years and it is great to see so many of those kids come back to work with us individually after that initial exposure. Our growth and improvement over the past couple of years has been amazing and I am just very proud to be a part of it here. Hockey has been such a huge part of my life, so to now be able to make my career doing what I love to do is incredible. And, to be able to give back to young people, that is so rewarding. Working with Robb is great too. He is a really good teacher and likes to see results. He realizes the

Laura Gieselman-Evanson

potential in goalies and he encourages them to work hard in order for them to achieve that. He lets the kids know exactly what they need to do so that they can improve, and then works with them until they reach their goals. He is very patient as well, which has a very positive effect on the kids."

ON WHY KIDS SHOULD COME TO THE GOALCREASE...

"What makes us so unique is that we are a year round academy with our own facility. Summer camps can't do what we do and that makes us very special. Then, we have such a great staff of instructors here, and they really care about the kids. We get to know the kids and we are like family in many ways. Because of that we can positively effect their lives both on and off the ice, which is very rewarding. Each teacher brings something unique to the table, yet we all come together with a common focus too. Our common bond is the fact that we all love kids and we obviously all love goaltending. Most importantly though, we have a passion for hockey and we love to have fun. The kids who come here love it and they love the environment. They get to have fun and hang out with other goalies, it is great. They can talk about their problems together, about their coaches, their teammates, their equipment or whatever, which is really nice for them. They build up their own support network and that can be a great thing."

ON WHY PARENTS SHOULD SEND THEIR KIDS HERE...

"I think that coming to the Goalcrease gives kids a distinct advantage over their competition. Beyond that, there are so many positive role models here that they are exposed to and that is so wonderful. The parents also get to know each other by coming here and hanging out during their kids' sessions. As a result, a lot of great friendships are made amongst them as well as a great support group of goalie parents. When they talk to each other about what their kids are going through and about the uniqueness of the position, it just makes life a lot easier. They share ideas and advice with each other too. Some of them even refer to the Goalcrease as their own 'club,' or community, which makes it very special for them. We enjoy hearing things like that."

ON TEACHING YOUNG GIRLS...

"I love it. To watch young girls progress and gain confidence in themselves is such a great thing. For girls, to have female goalie coaches is something that they really find to be a positive. The biggest compliment to me is when parents come up to me and tell me that their daughter wants to grow up and be just like me. I mean that is wonderful. We really get to make a difference in these kids' lives and that is so exciting. To help young girls realize their goals and dreams is so rewarding for me and for that I am very lucky to be able to do what I do. It is also cool to have a couple of girls who play Division I college hockey here with us because all of the younger girls can talk to them and watch them work out. They are great role models for them and they can learn so much from watching how they go about their business. Beyond that, it is great to see how quickly our girls pick things up here. When they are learning new things they are having success and when they have success they are having fun. That is what it is all about for us here at the Goalcrease."

JEFF HALL, FORMER BETHEL COLLEGE GOALIE & CURRENT GOALCREASE INSTRUCTOR

ON THE GENESIS OF THE GOALCREASE...

"I feel extremely lucky to be a part of the Goalcrease. This is a very unique place and a very unique opportunity for a young guy like myself to be able to do what I love to do. There are a very small number of people in the world who are lucky enough to make their living coaching goalies, and I am one of them. So, that is something I am very grateful for. Most goalie coaches have other part-time or full-time jobs on the side, which would be tough. All I ever wanted to do was play hockey and coach — that's why this job is a real dream come true for me.

Jeff Hall

"The way the Goalcrease has evolved has been a real pleasant surprise. It has taken off more so than I thought it would and I couldn't be happier. It has all just happened so quickly, which is great. I knew that there was a market out there for goalies who wanted to get more year round training, but to see how far we have come to make that a reality has been just awesome. To see these kids keep coming back year after year, at whatever level of hockey they are at, is so gratifying and that is what assures me that we are doing the right things here. The bottom line is that we owe all of our success to them because they are why we are here."

ON WHY PARENTS SHOULD SEND THEIR KIDS TO THE GOALCREASE:

"First and foremost, the Goalcrease is fun. That is by far the No. 1 reason why parents should send their kids to the Goalcrease. If you are going to spend $90 on a 40 minute session, then it had better be fun for your kids. That is a lot of money and you shouldn't spend it unless you are sure it will be fun and meaningful for them. I feel pretty safe in saying that probably more than 95% of the kids who come here have a blast. Having said that I would also say that the kids who come here are kids who really love hockey and who really want to get better at hockey. Defining what makes it "worth it" is a subjective thing, but certainly something that each family has to decide on their own. I would also say that parents shouldn't look at coming here as an investment for their son or daughter to get a college scholarship. That is a pretty rare and unique thing that requires a lot of dedication and hard work. Can it happen? Absolutely. But, for young kids I think the investment should be for them to come here and have fun while they are learning in a great, positive environment instead. If the scholarship happens, fine, but that can't be the focus.

"What I would also like parents to know about us is that we feel very strongly that kids need training. I am not saying come to us exclusively either, I am saying get your kid that extra training so they he or she can excel and have fun. That is what it is all about. For them to really get better they need to work at it outside of the team setting and ideally with a goalie coach who can work with them and help them to get better. Kids eventually figure out that if they come here and work with us that they are going to get a lot of attention and a lot of one-on-one instruction. The old mentality of kids just taking shot after shot in practice and then thinking that they are getting better is terrible. They need to get the proper instruction so that they learn how to stop shots the right way in order to get better as the game gets harder and faster."

ON THE VISION OF THE GOALCREASE:

"Just being a goalie, I think you have to have a solid perspective on life. You have to know how to deal with adversity probably more so than any other position in sports. The pressures that a goalie has to deal with are incredible. The amount of blame a goalie is given is too much for a lot of kids to handle. When we see kids start to take responsibility and stop make excuses when things go wrong, as a sort of defense mechanism, then we know that we are on the right track. I mean to watch the kids mature as a result of their hard work is just wonderful. Those things are tough and the kids who really excel at this position learn to deal with a lot of things that are thrown at them along the way. The kids who have a great attitude and can deal with those tough situations are the ones who will be successful not only in hockey, but in life. Goalies have to make the most of whatever is presented to them, and that can be tough.

"Let's say for instance that it is late in a game and a defenseman messes up and allows an opposing player to come in on a breakaway which will win the game if he scores. A lot of goalies are going to be scared out of their minds at that very moment. The good ones, however, the ones who are really learning those life lessons and are dealing with the adversity positively, are saying "all right, bring it on!" They can't wait for the opportunity to stop that shot and to accept that challenge head on. That is what we try to teach here, that confidence and that attitude, which can only be achieved through a lot of hard work and dedication. As teachers we recognize those things and really encourage it. So much of goaltending has to be experienced first hand, versus just explained in a book or out on the ice. Eventually kids realize that being scared is natural, but knowing how to react in that situation and how to deal with it is what matters most. Learning to hone that fear of failure is what we do best here. Now, will they stop the puck every time? No way. But if they do it right they will have success and most importantly, they will have fun. Seeing kids mature like that is so gratifying as a teacher and that is what keeps me coming back for more.

"We start with the basics here like being able to move around the crease; being able to bend your knees properly; and how to play the angles. Once kids master certain moves we move on to bigger and better things so that they gain more confidence and can taste success first hand. We also teach kids how to deal with frustration and pressure, which is invaluable in this position."

ON ROBB:

"Robb is a creative and intense guy. Those are the two words that immediately come to mind when I think of Robb. He is always thinking of new ideas and he is always trying to think of ways to make them come to life. Sometimes he is all over the map in doing that, but in the end he has a real passion for what he does and I really admire that. He loves to work with kids and he loves to educate people about how they can have more success at what they do."

CLINT ELBERTS, FORMER JUNIOR COLLEGE GOALIE & CURRENT GOALCREASE INSTRUCTOR

ON THE GENESIS OF THE GOALCREASE:

Clint Elberts

"I first met Robb when I was 12 years old and I attended the first Stauber-Ostby goalie camp. I was in awe of those guys. Before that I had been going all the way up to Canada every Summer to go to a camp. Once I attended Robb's camp though, I stopped going to Canada because I knew his was much better. Then, when I was 16, Robb asked me to work at some of his younger aged camps. I was flattered and had a lot of fun. Anyway, I kept working there during the Summers and eventually he approached me about working there full-time once he opened the Goalcrease. For me it was the opportunity of a life-time and I jumped at it. I get to affect kids in a positive way everyday here and that is what I like most about my job.

"To be a part of this whole dream from day one has been such a wild ride. I mean it started out with us going out and coaching at rinks all over the place. Then, when we finally got our own building so that kids could come to us, which was just wonderful. For me, to be a part of the initial creative process of starting this is so humbling. To think that many of my ideas were implemented and then brought to life is so cool. I will never forget how tough it was at the beginning either. I can remember being absolutely exhausted when we were trying to get everything done so that we could open the doors. We were sleeping here because there was just so much to do. From tearing up concrete to painting the walls to putting the ice in — it was an incredible journey to get from that point to where we are today. I am really proud of how far we have come and to just be a part of this whole thing. Without Robb I wouldn't have any of this and for that I am so grateful and thankful."

ON WHY PARENTS SHOULD SEND
THEIR KIDS TO THE GOALCREASE:

"The Goalcrease is an amazing place and if you send your kids here you will be giving them such a wonderful gift. Our staff is just second to none. We have so many people who played at so many different levels, from pro hockey in Europe; to the minor leagues; to the NHL; to college; to junior; to high school. That is just a lot of invaluable experience and we all have such a passion for the position. Not all of us made it as far as we would have liked to have gone, but I think it was more about the journey rather than the outcome that we enjoyed. So, now, to be able to pass that wisdom along to these kids is really neat. I think all of our different experiences add to the mix and we all have something very unique to say. I think we also all know where we made our mistakes, which gives us a lot of insight into teaching the position the right way. Most of us still have something to prove and this is an outlet for us to do that, through our students. We just want to teach them as best as we can so that they can have as much success as they are willing to work for in life. We are not a camp for goalies who want to be good, we are an academy where kids come who want to be great. There is a big difference. It is an incredible opportunity for kids who come here to get as much out of it as they want. As teachers we are willing to do whatever it takes for these kids, it is that important to us."

ON BEING A PART OF THE GOALCREASE TEAM:

"The most gratifying thing for me is to see a kid come in and work their butt off and then really improve to the point where they are really good. I remember one girl in particular who came in and after her third year with us I went to her section final high school game where she stopped 65 shots and then led her team to victory in overtime. That to me was better than any victory I ever had in my own life. You just get really attached to your kids here and when you see them do well it is so rewarding.

"You know, we have over 650 kids who come here now and we know them all. It is such a fun place and the kids love hanging out here. They make so many friends here and they absolutely love the positive environment that we have created for them. We even have kids who come in just to hang out, when they are not even scheduled for a session. They want to be here, to help shoot pucks or to talk to the other kids. They just love it here and that makes us feel pretty good about what we are doing."

ON ROBB:

"Robb is a very passionate person. The only reason that this place exists or that any of us are here is because of that passion. He is constantly thinking about goaltending, it is amazing. He is also constantly thinking about how he can make what we have even better. When he coaches kids there is no resting involved. He is constantly moving, constantly teaching and constantly working to make that kid better. He explains things in such a great way that kids really get it and that is half the battle right there. He gets in net and shows them how moves are broken down and then he challenges them to do it over and over again until they master it. He is just an awesome teacher."

ROBB HAS SERVED AS THE GOALIE COACH AT THE UNIVERSITY OF MINNESOTA SINCE 1999

The 2002 National Champion Gophers...

The 2003 National Champion Gophers...

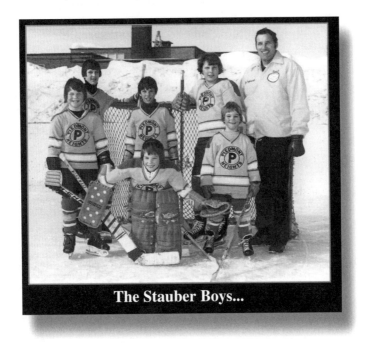

The Stauber Boys...

ROBB'S DAD, DELL

ON BEING PROUD OF YOUR SON...

"We are very proud of Robb, no question, but we have five more just like him and we are just as proud of them too."

ON MAKING SACRIFICES FOR YOUR KIDS...

"My wife Jean and I are very family oriented and we always felt that we could never spend enough time or do enough good things for our kids. That is what life is all about. We just did what we had to do in order to get by and that way we could spend a lot of our time doing what we felt was most important. We all worked very hard along the way but it was definitely a great ride. We didn't have a lot but we are certainly proud of all of our boys and their accomplishments."

ON ROBB AS A LITTLE KID...

"We knew that he was going to be something special right from the get-go. From the first time that little kid ever stepped on the ice we knew that he was going to be good. He made up his mind pretty early on too that he wanted to be a goalie. We gave him every opportunity to play other positions but he loved being a goalie, so that was his destiny I suppose. When Robb was growing up he was one of the most caring kids. He was always looking after somebody else and always interested in helping somebody. He just couldn't do enough for other people. He was also very close with his five brothers and still is to this day."

ON LIFE WITH SIX BOYS WHO ALL LOVED HOCKEY...

"With six boys all playing youth hockey it was an adventure, let me tell you. I don't know how many family meals we had together during those days, because we were always on the go. Whether it was practice or a game or a tournament on the road, we were always on the move. I would pack up my car and go one way while my wife packed up her car and headed the other way. Those were the days. Even though I didn't play much hockey myself as a kid, I got involved with it through the boys. I was the rink director at Piedmont Heights for many years; I coached several teams during that time; and I was also a member of the Duluth Amateur Hockey Association too. So, I took an interest in it and made the most of it. It was all worth it too because all of our boys went on to become just outstanding kids not to mention outstanding hockey players. When the kids were finally in college, those were the best years of our lives. It was like a reward for all of that hard work. To be able to drive down and see them play in that environment was just wonderful. I was so proud of all of them. To know that five of the six kids got to go to college because of hockey was just icing on the cake. We always made sure that their studies came first though, and then hockey came second. They were all very hard workers both in school as well as on the ice, so we were just lucky I suppose to have such great kids."

ON ROBB MAKING IT IN THE NHL...

"When Robb got drafted into the NHL we were so pleased. We were there with him when it happened and it was very emotional. I mean how many parents get the opportunity to see their kids play at that level, not very many. That stretch of his life was a lot of fun too, traveling around and watching his games. To see him on TV playing alongside Wayne Gretzky, and things like that, you can't even describe how proud that makes you feel as a parent. Jean and I traveled out to L.A. quite a bit to see his games and his teammates always made us feel very welcome. It was a lot of fun to be around those types of people. They were good people and that was nice to see."

ON ROBB'S SUCCESS AT THE GOALCREASE...

"Now, to see Robb having success with the Goalcrease is just wonderful. We are tickled pink for him and for his success. Robb is an excellent teacher and is so good with kids. He is not a holler and screamer like his dad, he truly has the patience of a saint. He demands excellence though and really wants to get the best out of his kids. He is very even tempered too, which makes him very approachable to his students. He is very positive and upbeat about all of his kids and loves them all like they were his own. You know, Robb's success hasn't changed him a bit either. He is still the same lovable kid he always was. We still talk to him on the phone probably every day or every other day and remain very close with him. We are very interested in what he is doing and feel great about the success he is having with his career. He remains very close with his brothers too, and that is just great to see as well. They all help each other out and are real close-knit. As a parent that is also very gratifying. So, we couldn't be happier for him and wish him nothing but the best — he truly deserves it."

ROBB'S MOM, JEAN

ON ROBB'S LOVE OF HOCKEY...

"Robb was bound and determined to be a goalie from a very young age. He loved it then and he caries that same passion for the position even to this day. It was just amazing watching him grow up and become such a talented player. Seeing him play at the University of Minnesota was great and when he was drafted into the NHL we were all so proud. Then, to be able to go out and visit him and watch his games in Los Angeles, that was such a thrill. It was just a real joy, his entire career."

ON BEING A GOALIE MOM...

"Being a goalie mom was stressful at times, no question. I definitely did better watching him on TV than in person though. Watching him play in person was so nerve racking, I am sure I dug my elbows into the people on both sides of me pretty hard during those games. You learn to deal with the negative things though, like what fans might yell from the stands, and to just tune it out. It is not for the weak of heart, that is for sure."

ON THE SECRET OF ROBB'S SUCCESS...

"I would have to say it is because he had a terrific mother, but then again I am a little biased! Really though, Robb is a great teacher because he has a very positive attitude. He gets the best out of kids by being positive rather than being negative, which is the opposite of what so many other coaches do. He finds the best qualities in kids and he pulls that out of them to make them better. He has a real gift as a teacher and that is why his business has been so successful. Robb just works so hard and has so much confidence, that is why he will find success in whatever he does. He has a very strong work ethic and do you know what? I think he got that from his mom and dad."

ON RAISING SIX HOCKEY PLAYERS...

"I have had a lifetime of hockey raising six boys and just when I thought it was finally over, I was blessed with a whole bunch of hockey-loving grandchildren. So, I am still out there standing in snow banks watching games after all these years. Once hockey gets in your blood it is in you forever. It was something that definitely made our family stronger over the years though and I am very proud of the fact that five of the six went on to play in college. More importantly, all of them went to college. So, to be able to get your education and do what you love at the same time — that is just wonderful."

ROBB'S BROTHER, JOHN

WHAT KIND OF A GUY IS YOUR BROTHER ROBB?

"You know, I am just very proud of him. Robb comes from a very modest middle-class hard working family and he has represented us with pride. His work ethic and modesty are amazing and he has accomplished so much for being so young. With six brothers it is pretty tough to get a big head though, so Robb has remained humble through it all and we are proud of him. The bottom line is that Robb is just a good brother."

WHAT KIND OF A TEACHER IS ROBB?

"As a teacher Robb is great. I mean he was meant to teach. I really enjoy watching him teach young kids and help them get better at hockey. He has so much patience. It is amazing how patient he is with those kids. I see that with his own children as well, he is a very good father. His work ethic is unbelievable too. I mean you will not find many guys who will work harder that Robb. He is extremely positive and always has a great attitude about life. Even in the worst of times he is somehow able to find the positives out of it. He is also extremely thorough almost to the point where he is really anal. I mean that in a good way, he is just very organized and on top of stuff. You know, Robb is one of the fiercest competitors I have ever known and I think that is why he is so successful."

ON THE GOALCREASE...

"I guess what I would say to parents of young goaltenders is that I think it is a very small investment in your child's future with a guaranteed pay-off. And when I say pay-off I mean both on and off the ice because Robb teaches kids not only about hockey but about life. Robb realizes that not every kid is going to be a superstar. He gets that. So, he just tries to get kids to play to the best of their abilities."

YOUR FAVORITE ROBB STORY...

"Sorry, I know kids will be reading this book so I don't think we can put it in the there!"

ROBB'S BROTHER, JAMIE

WHAT KIND OF A GUY IS YOUR BROTHER ROBB?

"Robb is a very kind and generous person. He honestly cares a lot about people. He is also a very wise person, just a really smart guy. He is an easygoing and fun guy too. He never gets too emotional around the kids he is teaching and always remains very calm and patient with them. Robb is also very competitive, no matter what it is he is doing. He is driven too, so much so that he wants to succeed in everything he does. He is a very determined guy and has been that way forever. So, I am very proud of him. He is a very successful person and he deserves it too, because nobody works harder."

WHAT KIND OF A TEACHER IS ROBB?

"What Robb has that a lot of other teachers and coaches don't have is an extreme passion to help kids improve and reach their potential. He just loves kids and honestly wants to help them both on and off the ice. When you talk to Robb you can just sense the energy and enthusiasm in him. He has been that way since he was a little kid and it is great to see him be able to use that for something so wonderful at the Goalcrease."

ON THE GOALCREASE...

"I think that the Goalcrease is probably the premier instructional and developmental program for goalies in the country. I say that not only because Robb is my brother, but also because I have seen a lot of the other camps that are out there and met a lot of the goalie coaches. The individual instruction that he gives his kids is just second to none. He and his entire staff are so dedicated and concerned about their goalies and that is so great to see. Robb has his staff so focused on what he wants to teach them and he really makes sure that they are all on the same page for how they want to teach each kid. It is a really impressive operation they have going over there."

YOUR FAVORITE ROBB STORY...

"You know, my favorite story about Robb happened just this past Fourth of July up here in Duluth. We got to spend a week together at the lake with our families and it was just wonderful. I got to see Robb the father that week versus Robb the coach or Robb the player, and it was great. Our kids had so much fun together. He is so good with his kids as well as with all of his nieces and nephews, they just love him. I think that is way more impressive than anything he has ever done in hockey to tell you the truth."

ROBB'S BROTHER, DAN

WHAT KIND OF A GUY IS YOUR BROTHER ROBB?

"Robb is a very caring and passionate person. He is very sincere too, just an overall great person. He is one of the hardest working guys I know and that is why he has always been successful. I have always admired his work ethic and his positive attitude. He has always been a great brother and is very supportive of our interests as well. Robb wants all of his friends and family to be successful, that is just the way he is. I am proud of him, he has done so well for himself and that is just great to see."

WHAT KIND OF A TEACHER IS ROBB?

"As a teacher, Robb is very passionate. All teachers have to be passionate in order to be successful, and that is Robb to a tee. He is extremely knowledgeable about hockey and about goaltending, so he is a natural as a coach. In fact, I don't think he gets enough credit for his coaching ability. I have been coaching at the college level for a lot of years now and I don't know many coaches smarter than he is. I think he would make a fantastic D-I coach because he is just that intelligent about the game. Goaltenders see the game differently, from the net on out, and they have a different perspective about the game much the same way a quarterback in football does. He has so much patience too, which is a real gift."

ON THE GOALCREASE...

"Robb demands excellence from those around him and he expects people to work hard who come to the Goalcrease. So, it is not a Summer fun camp by any stretch. It is such an incredible place though, just a fantastic learning environment for goaltenders. As a parent and coach I would highly recommend it, it is absolutely worth it. If kids come in and listen to Robb's philosophy on how to play the position and then work hard, they will be successful. And in my book, what is successful is not necessarily how many games you win, but rather how you develop as a player and as a person. When Robb works with kids he tries to instill a passion in them and tries to develop their leadership skills. So, in that regard, Robb and the Goalcrease are invaluable."

YOUR FAVORITE ROBB STORY...

"First of all, Robb and I look a lot alike. OK, back in 1988, when Robb was playing in the Frozen Four out in Lake Placid, some funny things happened to him... er me I guess. I flew out there with some buddies to watch Robb and my brother Pete, who was also there playing with Lake Superior State. Anyway, when the Gophers lost in the opening round to St. Laurence, there were some rumors circulating around in the media that the reason the Gophers lost was because Robb had been out partying too late the night before the game. Well, funny, but that wasn't Robb, that was me!

"That was the first funny part about the story. The second part is that while I was out there partying I got approached by an NHL agent who wanted to take me to breakfast that next morning to talk about signing a pro contract. I said 'Sure, breakfast sounds great!' This guy just assumed that I was Robb so I decided to have some fun with him. Finally, after a nice big meal, I told him that I thought the most important thing for an agent to do was to really know who his client was. That was when I proceeded to tell him that I was Robb's brother. He just looked at me in utter disbelief, it was hilarious. Ironically though, that agent, Art Kaminsky, wound up working with both of us — I signed with him to play over in Europe and Robb later signed with him when he played with the L.A. Kings. That breakfast turned out to be money well spent I suppose. He never confused the two of us after that though!"

ROBB'S BROTHER, PETE

WHAT KIND OF A GUY IS YOUR BROTHER ROBB?

"Robb is just a really good guy. First and foremost he is a great father and a wonderful brother. We are very close and I think the world of him. Robb is very gracious and humble and I am so proud of his success, he totally deserves it. His success never changed him a bit either. He is still the same guy around us and I respect him a lot for that. Of course he knows that if he ever did get too cocky around us he would have five brothers to knock him down to where he belongs! We are all close as brothers though and none of us think we are better than anybody else. We all support each other and stay in touch with each other and that is really nice."

WHAT KIND OF A TEACHER IS ROBB?

"I have seen Robb working at his camps and he has such a strong work ethic. He does an excellent job with those kids. He really emphasizes the fundamentals with them and has so much patience. You know, Robb was always so intense as an athlete, he just hated to lose. I think he brings that same intensity to his teaching too. He just really wants to win at everything he does and that includes giving his kids the best education possible."

ON THE GOALCREASE...

"The Goalcrease is just awesome, and I am not just saying that because I am his brother. It is truly amazing. I would highly recommend it for anybody who wants their kid to learn from a teacher who truly cares. I mean Robb has emerged as one of the top goalie coaches in the country and I don't think anybody could dispute that. You know, I think a lot of guys have gotten into the hockey camp business lately just to make a quick buck, but Robb is in it for the long haul. He wants to make young goaltenders better and really make a difference in their lives. He realizes that they are the most neglected players on their teams and wanted to do something about it."

YOUR FAVORITE ROBB STORY...

"OK, one of the most memorable times I ever had with Robb happened back in college in 1988 when I played at Lake Superior State University and Robb was with the Gophers. We both made it to the NCAA Frozen Four out in Lake Placid, New York, and got to spend some time together out there. We never faced each other though because Minnesota got beat in the opening round by St. Laurence and we went on to win it all that year. But I will never forget that experience of being out there together at such a meaningful time in our lives. Two kids from Duluth playing in the Final Four, it was a great moment. I will say, however, that I am absolutely certain if Minnesota had beaten St. Laurence and met us in the Finals, we would have won that game too! Really though, to win a National Championship was so amazing, but to have my brother there with me made it just that much more special.

"Another moment I will never let him forget happened back in high school in 1984, my senior year, in the section final game against St. Cloud Apollo. I have said it before and I will say it again, Robb lost the game for us which would have sent us to the state tournament. He let a slap-shot in from outside the blue line late in the third period and that sealed the deal. I was devastated. I mean the thing just floated up there. My four year old could have stopped that puck for crying out loud! I am just kidding about it being his fault of course, but I will never let him live that down for as long he lives."

ROBB'S BROTHER, BILL

WHAT KIND OF A GUY IS YOUR BROTHER ROBB?

"I wouldn't trade him for anything in the world, how's that? There are just so many positive qualities about Robb. He is very caring, very generous and his heart is always in the right place. He is a great listener. He is the eternal optimist too because he always has an upbeat attitude about everything. You can always count on him for help if you need him too. He is definitely a very loving and trustworthy friend. I am very proud of his success both on and off the ice. He is a successful hockey player, coach, father and businessman. He has found a niche that is just perfect for him and I wish him nothing but the best. What more can I say, he is my brother and I love him."

WHAT KIND OF A TEACHER IS ROBB?

"He is a great teacher. I have worked at a few of his goalie camps with him over the years and it was fun to see him beyond being my brother and as a coach. I worked at the camp as a shooter, meaning I was there to shoot pucks at the goalies and work with them. Well, I learned so much about goaltending from Robb doing that, it was amazing. He makes it so simple that it is hard not to understand stuff with him. He breaks things down step by step and then is able to communicate with the kids in a way that they get it. For instance, when you get a math problem wrong it is difficult for the teacher to explain why it is wrong. If you don't get it, you don't get it, and you will probably never get the answer right. Well, with Robb he can show the goalies how to do things the right way. He will get in net with the kids and show them exactly what they are doing wrong and then show them how to correct it. Visually, that is so powerful as a learning tool. It was just so neat to see these kids improving right before your very eyes, gaining confidence and getting better as they went along."

ON THE GOALCREASE...

"I know that it is an expensive camp. But, if I had a son or daughter who wanted to be a goaltender, I don't think I could afford not to send them there. I say this because I have seen the camp up close and personal. It is an amazing facility with an amazing staff. You know, it's funny but so often parents will spend thousands of dollars on new goalie pads and fancy painted masks, but they don't get them the basic fundamental instruction that they really need more than anything. So, in my opinion it would be a fantastic investment in your kids' future to send them to see Robb and learn the position from an expert who really enjoys teaching."

YOUR FAVORITE ROBB STORY...

"I remember one time in high school Robb and I got into an argument and it got pretty heated. I was the youngest of six boys and Robb was the second youngest so we were always battling for seniority. Well, mom always said that if we were going to fight then we had better get the heck outside so we didn't break anything. So, we both went outside and squared up to battle like men. As we were eyeing each other over and waiting to see who was going to throw the first punch, I distracted him by looking over his shoulder and saying hello to a friend of ours who I pretended to be there. Robb, being the nice guy that he was, didn't want to be rude so he turned around to say hello too. When he turned back after realizing that nobody was there, he was greeted with a fistful of knuckles. Whack! He didn't see it coming and he just buckled at the knees. The fight was over before it even started. I felt awful. You know, with five older brothers sometimes you had to get creative. I still feel bad about that to this day, so I want to officially say 'Sorry big bro!' "

The Teacher...

THE STAUBER BROTHERS:

WHERE ARE THEY NOW?

John owns a lumber business in Duluth. (Never played college hockey.)

Jamie is a pilot in the National Guard in Duluth and also runs Stauber Brothers Sporting Goods. (Played at UM-Duluth.)

Dan is the head hockey coach at the University of Wisconsin, Superior. (Played at UW-Superior.)

Pete is a police officer. (Played at Lake Superior State University.)

Robb owns and operates the Goalcrease. (Played for Gophers, NHL.)

Bill is a police officer. (Played Junior Hockey and later played briefly for UM-Duluth.)

GOALCREASE MISSION-STATEMENT

We will continually bring to market safe, effective and innovative training services, training facilities, training tools, and custom-fit equipment for hockey goalies of every age and level of competition. We will strive to increase every goalie's self-esteem and help them reach their stated objectives.

CHAPTER TWELVE:
ABOUT THE GOALCREASE

Stopping the puck… it's every goalies bottom line. Achieving that objective on any kind of consistent basis, however, is anything but simple. This is why Robb Stauber founded Goalcrease, Inc. The Goalcrease is exclusively devoted to perfecting and innovating the arts and sciences of hockey goalkeeping. As a result, we're closer than ever to helping goalies at every level of competition realize their full potential and personal ambitions. The Goalcrease strives to innovate, develop, and bring to the hockey world new and better ways to train and prepare hockey goalies.

One-on-one goalie training at the Goalcrease is incomparable. Our ability to improve a goalie's skills and self-confidence is unparalleled. While this type of high-quality and individualized training has been accessible to athletes like golfers and tennis players for many, many years, it's never been readily accessible to hockey goalies. Now goalies at every level of competition can receive personal training on real ice and personal video analysis from world-class instructors at the Goalcrease Training Center. Hundreds of goalies from the United States and Canada have already discovered the Goalcrease training advantage for themselves and their teams. Goalies located within a 150-200 mile radius are choosing to train at the Goalcrease on a regular basis, while goalies from other parts of the U.S. and Canada are concentrating their training in a one and/or two week period.

THE GOALCREASE'S
TRAINING PHILOSOPHIES:

We believe a positive environment nurtures learning . . . we believe in quality over quantity . . . we believe personalized attention is the best way to take into account each student's learning style and playing style.

Goalcrease trainers are trained to identify and respect your individual playing style, to build on your strengths, and to eliminate your weaknesses. On the ice, your instructor will be constantly teaching, demonstrating, reinforcing personal strengths, and constructively correcting mistakes as soon as they're spotted. There's no shot quota at the Goalcrease Training Center. We want every save to be a good save which means we're patient and skilled at correcting problems. In your video sessions, the training tips and corrections from the preceding ice session will be reviewed and reinforced. Slow motion/stop action is frequently used to break down every movement so that students can see bad habits being broken as well as good habits being developed.

OVERALL, EVERY CERTIFIED GOALCREASE TRAINER IS CAREFULLY AND THOUGHTFULLY TAUGHT TO ACHIEVE SPECIFIC TRAINING GOALS:

- *Create a positive learning environment*
- *Treat each student respectfully and individually*
- *Expect respectful behavior from each student*
- *Accommodate and teach different styles of goalkeeping*
- *Enhance and reinforce each goalie's individual strengths*
- *Focus on the basic fundamentals of goalkeeping*
- *Repeat those basic fundamentals*
- *Provide immediate correction – constructively*
- *Turn the basic fundamentals into habit*
- *Turn hockey lessons into life lessons when applicable*

AT THE GOALCREASE, WE UNDERSTAND THE ANGLES...

Goaltending is a position based on geometry and mathematical probability. We must teach the goalie from the prospective of the puck to be successful. There are three components of the angle system that a goalie must learn to perform at their best. The first two are angles, Lateral and Aerial Angles. The third component is Depth, how far out of the net to play on any given situation.

The Lateral Angle is the more obvious of the two. Its net entry width varies based on the location of the puck on the ice. When the puck is centered on the net its maximum net entry width is six feet. As the puck moves away from the center of the net the entry width decreases.

The Aerial Angle is always fixed at the net height of four feet. Although its height does not change it is misunderstood more than the lateral angle. The Aerial Angle is harder to visualize. Goaltenders should approach the position from this perspective. Goalie coaches must instruct the position from the puck's perspective rather than the Shooter's Eyes.

Another important aspect of playing the angles is Angle Depth. Angle depth is how close or how far the goalie is away from the puck when the shot is taken. It is referenced from the net. The closer to the puck you are the more net you cover. The amount of depth a goalie plays is dictated by the game situation. However, challenging a shooter too much is as bad, if not worst than not enough. Goalies who have poor footwork skills generally play the extremes in regards to depth.

DEVELOPMENT

Certified Instruction + Real Ice + Video Analysis + Pro Shop

HOW DO GOALIES GET BETTER DURING THE OFF-SEASON?

They train. And, the best available summer training opportunity is a week or two at the Goalcrease Summer Academy. There are five Goalcrease Summer Academy programs to choose from: Introductory, Intermediate, Advanced, Elite and Goalcrease Prospects. All five programs offer a maximum four-to-one student to coach ratio and no session has more than 24 goalies. Each program is available to both females and males and has been carefully designed and refined over many years of successful implementation. Our certified and experienced instructors are among the very best in the world and carefully taught to create a positive learning environment.

GOALCREASE TRAINING TOOLS

The drive that made Robb Stauber a successful goalie at every level of hockey inspires Goalcrease Inc. to research and develop goalie-specific training tools. Some basic assumptions drive the R&D process. First, an athlete who learns the feeling for 'doing it right' has the best opportunity for long-term success. Second, it's easier to teach an athlete good habits, than it is to break their bad habits. Third, muscles have memory. Therefore, if a goalie's function is to block flying pucks, then it makes sense that the goalie should understand: 1.) the form and shape that yields the most blocked shots; 2.) what that form and shape feels like; and 3.) how to teach muscles to automatically remember that form and shape. Bingo! The advent of Goalcrease Training Tools.

THE GOALCREASE CUSTOM-FIT PRO SHOP

We hire only one kind of person to work at Stauber's Goalcrease Custom-Fit Pro Shop. And, that kind of person is another goalkeeper who has been carefully trained to fit goalie equipment. At Stauber's Goalcrease Custom-Fit Pro Shop we know how to fit you with the safest, best fitting, most appropriate goalie equipment based on your playing needs and playing style. If that equipment isn't available as a stock item, we'll take every measure possible to get it custom-made. Stauber's Goalcrease Custom-Fit Pro Shop handles most major brands of goalie equipment at the lowest prices possible. We carry the following manufacturers: CCM, RBK, Koho, Vaughn, Brown, Bauer, Itech, Eddy and Christian Brothers. So, why buy your goalie equipment from a sporting goods store clerk who might really know aluminum bats, but who has never even heard of a thigh board?

MEET THE GOALCREASE STAFF:

PAUL OSTBY, DIRECTOR OF TRAINING

Paul was a standout goalie at the University of Minnesota and was voted MVP of the 1982 Golden Gopher hockey team. Paul was selected for two National Olympic Festivals and played on the 1982-83 U.S. National Team that won the World B Pool Gold Medal in Tokyo, Japan. Paul later attended the New York Rangers training camp in 1982, but was later forced to retire when a severe ankle injury ended his playing career in 1984.

From 1984-86, Paul coached the USHL St. Paul Vulcan goalies, three of whom received Division I scholarships. He then went on to serve as the goalie coach at the University of Minnesota from 1986-93. Three of Paul's goalies went on to play the NHL. (Incidentally, one of his star pupils during his tenure in Gold Country was a kid named Robb Stauber.) Paul later coached at Apple Valley High School from 1994-96, winning the Minnesota "AA" State Championship in 1995-96. After serving as the Director of Goaltending for Shattuck-St. Mary's Academy (Faribault, MN.), that next year, Paul took over as the goalkeeper coach for Benilde-St. Margaret High School, the 1998-99 and 2000-01 Minnesota Class "A" State Champions.

In addition to working as the Director of Training at Goalcrease, Paul has worked with Minnesota based hockey agent Neal Sheehy for the past six years and recently became a certified agent in the Fall of 2005.

CLINT ELBERTS

Clint Elberts played for Lakeville High School (Minn.) from 1997–00 and then spent the 2001-02 season playing junior hockey for the Portland Pioneers. Clint has been a student of Robb Stauber and Paul Ostby since 1992 and has been a certified Goalcrease instructor since 1999. Clint made significant contributions to the research and development of The Staubar Trainer and continues to develop innovative tools for application in training goalies.

LAURA GIESELMAN-EVANSON

A 2003 graduate of St. Cloud State University, Laura Gieselman-Evanson earned B.S. degrees in Sports Management and Marketing, along with a minor in Athletic Coaching. Laura also starred between the pipes for the Division I Lady Huskies, even serving as the team captain as a senior. Among her many honors and accolades, Laura received the Most Valuable Player award, the Academic Achievement award and was selected "Star of the Season" by the St. Cloud Times. A three year on-ice hockey camp counselor at Shattuck St. Mary's. Laura trained with Robb and Paul for more than five years. She has been a certified Goalcrease instructor since 2003.

ANDREW KENT

Andy Kent played high school hockey at Lakeville (Minn.) from 2000-2002 and then spent the 2002-2003 season with the Twin Cities Northern Lights team. Andy has been a Stauber/Ostby goalie for over 10 years now, and has been a certified Goalcrease instructor since 2001.

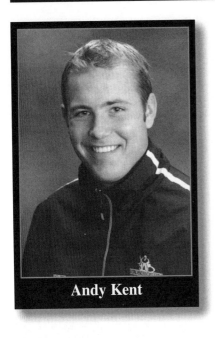

Andy Kent

STEVE DEBUS

Steve DeBus played for Rochester Mayo High School (Minn.) and then went on to play for the USHL's Rochester Mustangs from 1991-1993. From there, DeBus had a very distinguished four-year career at the University of Minnesota, garnering All-WCHA honors in 1997. With degrees in Natural Resources and American Indian Studies, Steve became a certified Goalcrease instructor in 2004.

JEFF HALL

Jeff Hall played for Edina High School (Minn.) from 1996–98 and was in the nets when the Hornets won the 1997 "AA" Minnesota State High School Championship. An All-State tournament team selection in 1997, Jeff earned Classic Lake All-Conference honors as well as All-State Honorable Mention honors in 1998. Jeff went on to play collegeiately at Bethel College in St. Paul, where, in addition to earning a degree in Physical Education, he received the prestigious Coach's Award in both 2001 and 2002. Jeff has been a certified goalie instructor at the Goalcrease since 1998.

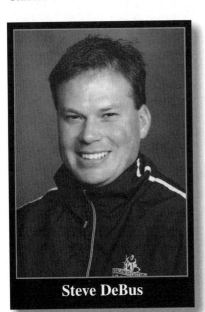

Steve DeBus

LISA JACK, PH.D., LP

Lisa Jack is the Goalcrease Consulting Sports Psychologist. Lisa brings a rich and varied 10 year background in human development, leadership development, and stress management which she gained in both academia and business. Lisa received her M.S. and Ph.D in Counseling Psychology from the University of Southern California, L.A.

ROBB STAUBER, BY THE NUMBERS...

Among Robb's many honors and accolades, he was the first goaltender ever to receive the Hobey Baker Memorial Award, emblematic of the nation's top collegiate player, in 1988. That same year Robb was named as a first team All-American as well as the WCHA Player of the Year while at the University of Minnesota. Robb also received the Gopher's John Mariucci Most Valuable Player Award that season as well. As for the record book, he rewrote much of it, starting with the single-season record for games played (44), followed by minutes played (2,621), saves (1,711) and shutouts (5) in 1987-88. Robb also holds the Gopher career record for save percentage (.906), but fell to No. 2 in games played (98), minutes played (5,717) and wins (73), thanks to his protégé, Adam Hauser. During Stauber's stellar career in Gold Country, the team posted a 102-34-4 record, back-to-back WCHA Championships in 1987-88 and 1988-89, and three-straight NCAA Frozen Four appearances. As a professional, Robb was well known as an offensive-minded netminder with a unique style all his own. In all, Robb scored 12 points over his decade-long pro career (1 goal & 11 assists).

ROBB'S CAREER STATS

Season	Team	League	GP	W	L	T	SO	Avg
1984-85	Duluth-Denfeld Wildcats	MSHSL	22					1.70
1985-86	Duluth-Denfeld Wildcats	MSHSL	27					3.26
1986-87	University of Minnesota	WCHA	20	13	5	0	0	3.53
1986-87	United States	WJC-A	4					4.64
1987-88	University of Minnesota	WCHA	44	34	10	0	5	2.72
1988-89	University of Minnesota	WCHA	34	26	8	0	0	2.43
1988-89	United States	WEC-A	6	3	3	0	0	3.64
1989-90	Los Angeles Kings	NHL	2	0	1	0	0	7.95
1989-90	New Haven Nighthawks	AHL	14	6	6	2	0	3.03
1990-91	New Haven Nighthawks	AHL	33	13	16	4	1	3.67
1990-91	Phoenix Roadrunners	IHL	4	1	2	0	0	4.13
1991-92	Phoenix Roadrunners	IHL	22	8	12	1	0	3.86
1992-93	Los Angeles Kings	NHL	31	15	8	4	0	3.84
1993-94	Los Angeles Kings	NHL	22	4	11	5	1	3.41
1993-94	Phoenix Roadrunners	IHL	3	1	1	0	0	6.42
1994-95	Los Angeles Kings	NHL	1	0	0	0	0	7.50
1994-95	Buffalo Sabres	NHL	6	2	3	0	0	3.79
1995-96	Rochester Americans	AHL	16	6	7	1	0	3.53
1996-97	Portland Pirates	AHL	30	13	13	2	0	3.06
1997-98	Hartford Wolf Pack	AHL	39	20	10	6	2	2.40
1998-99	Manitoba Moose	IHL	5	2	1	1	0	4.78
NHL Totals			**62**	**21**	**23**	**9**	**1**	**3.80**

SO... WHAT'S IT REALLY LIKE TO BE A GOALTENDER?

The great Jacques Plante, who introduced the mask to modern goaltending after being cut badly by a shot to the face, summed it up this way:

"Imagine sitting at your desk. You make a mistake. A red light goes on behind you, a siren starts sounding and 18,000 people are yelling at you. That's what it's like to be a goaltender..."

I couldn't agree more!

See you on the ice... Thanks!